RE-PITCHING THE TENT

RE-PITCHING THE TENT

Re-ordering the church building for worship and mission

'And whenever the cloud was taken
up from over the tent, after that the
people of Israel set out; and in the
place where the cloud settled down,
there the people of Israel encamped.'
Numbers 9.17

RICHARD GILES

Revised and expanded edition

Illustrations by Roy Barnes

Foreword by The Archbishop of York

A Liturgical Press Book

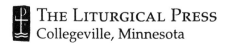
THE LITURGICAL PRESS
Collegeville, Minnesota

ISBN 0 8146 2709 9

*Typeset by Rowland Phototypesetting Limited,
Bury St Edmunds, Suffolk
and printed in Great Britain by
St Edmundsbury Press Limited,
Bury St Edmunds, Suffolk*

This book is respectfully dedicated to
Pere Frederic Debuyst OSB,
the master

FOREWORD

By The Archbishop of York

Richard Giles has given the church an invaluable handbook in *Re-Pitching the Tent*. Its immense flexibility is one of its greatest attractions as is his passionate style of writing.

The book reflects his eagerness for the things of God to be reflected both in building and in people.

In drawing on his wide learning and experience his writing is always interesting, if at times properly provocative, as he seeks to excite in the local church a renewal of its life in Christ and a more effective proclamation of the Gospel, not only through the worship of the living stones, but also through the bricks and mortar, the layout and design of the church building itself.

+ David Ebor

ACKNOWLEDGEMENTS

I wish to record my sincere thanks to the very special people without whom this book would not have been written:

Bishop Michael Marshall for constant encouragement;

Fr Roger Davison for the curacy where it all began;

John Bunker who first opened my eyes to what was possible;

Ron and Margaret Carbutt and Elvi Rhodes for their generosity;

Nigel Dees and Paul Walker for helping the second edition to become more user-friendly to readers from the Roman Catholic community;

Fr Michael Komechak OSB and David Philippart for showing me the beautiful and exciting things the Church is doing in Greater Chicago;

Fr Ivan Marchesin and the Xaverian Missionaries of East Hyde Park Boulevard, Chicago for showing me how to move in worship;

John Morrison, Jim Postell and Tom Wray for introducing me to the Diocese of Southern Ohio;

Gerry Pottebaum and Bill Shickell for showing me Loveland, Ohio;

the Benedictines of the abbeys of St Procopius Illinois, La Pierre-Qui-Vire, Fleury and Clerlande, for giving me fresh vision as well as gracious hospitality;

Tony and Audrey Pinkney for sharing their haven in the Perigord Blanc;

Robin and Jan Sayer for the use of 'Captain Scott's hut' at the bottom of their garden;

Susan and Simone for making it possible for me to disappear for three months;

and the people of St Thomas' Huddersfield for putting up with an absentee priest.

'I shall take a building. A building shaped like a cross, furnished neither for habitation nor defence. I shall multiply this building by a thousand, by ten thousand, by a hundred thousand. It may be as small as a single room; it may soar into the sky. It may be old or it may be new; it may be plain or it may be rich; it may be of stone or it may be of wood or it may be of brick or of mud. This building is in the heart of cities and it is in the wild places of earth. It is on islands and in deserts and upon mountains. It is in Provence and Suffolk and Tuscany and Alsace and in Vermont and Bolivia and the Lebanon. The walls and furnishings of this building tell stories; they talk of kings and queens and angels and devils; they instruct and they threaten. They are intended to uplift and terrify. They are an argument made manifest.'

Rose Macaulay
The Towers of Trebizond

'It's never stopped changing and we wouldn't be on the air now, in my view, if it hadn't changed and evolved and, if it doesn't keep on evolving, it will die.'

David Liddiment, Executive Producer 'Coronation Street'

'Surely all art is the result of having been in danger, of having gone through an experience all the way to the end, to where no one can go any further.'

Rainer Maria Rilke

'La vrai mission du vitrail n'est pas de nous apporter serenité de confort spirituel, mais de nous plonger a nouveau dans l'aventure du Supernaturel.'

Jean-Balzaine, L'église St Severin, Paris

CONTENTS

PREFACE

Have you ever been to an Anglican service of Institution and Induction of a new parish priest – the kind of liturgy which, every time you think the last hymn has arrived, lurches into (what passes for) life with that most dreaded of liturgical tortures, the intercessions?

Attendance at such services is an occupational hazard for clergy, and for as long as I can remember, I have relieved the monotony of these occasions by carrying out in my mind's eye an extensive re-ordering of the building concerned; what I would do if only I could get my hands on it! The whole process, from the gutting of the church building through its refurbishment to the grand re-opening is achieved within the space of an hour and under the very nose of the archdeacon.

The backs of countless hymn sheets had been covered in scribbles and scrawls of new sanctuaries and seating plans, and the more 'impossible' the building the greater the fun.

Then in 1987 came the offer from Bishop David Hope (now Archbishop) to go on doodling, but this time it was to be official. I was given the remit of scribbling and scrawling for the parishes of the Wakefield Diocese, helping them to dream dreams of how their buildings might be improved and adapted to help Christians today operate more effectively in a part of the world where in 1993 less than 2% of the adult population was involved with the Church on a regular basis.

To clip my wings in my flights of fancy, I was 'earthed' into a tiny urban parish where I was given an immediate opportunity (in the shape of a gloomy and over-large Victorian 'masterpiece') to put into practice in my own back yard the gospel that I was to preach to others.

Over the last eleven years it has been exciting to witness the surge of interest in church re-ordering in the Wakefield Diocese, and to see with my own eyes the many successful projects which have turned parishes around and given fresh hope to all concerned.

Here and there my doodles have come in handy, but again and again members of parish communities wanting to re-order but not knowing where to begin, ask the question 'How can we make a start?' and 'What is there for us to read?' It is in response to these needs that this handbook has been prepared.

Sadly, the ground-breaking works of Peter Hammond and of The New Churches Research Group are out of print; the Birmingham Institute of Liturgy and Architecture, pioneered by Gilbert Cope and J G Davies is no more, and although there exists some excellent new material of a technical nature,* there is little that covers the middle ground where theology and spatial design meet and interact. Only the specialist periodicals – notably *Church Building* in England, and *Environment and Art* in the United States – keep the flag flying.

Martin Purdy produced in 1991 a comprehensive technical design guide for those engaged in the design of places of worship.
Churches & Chapels, Butterworth Architecture 1991

This handbook is offered as a 'doodler's resource book' for all those – whether clergy, architects, church council members or just good plain honest faithful – who strive to make sense of the Church's built inheritance at a time when the world sets out from a different starting point than when these stones were first raised.

It is designed to be equally suitable for individual reading or for group study. It can be read right through, or used selectively as a resource book.

The three sections of the book approach the question of re-ordering our church buildings under the headings of the three basic questions which every community of faith needs to ask itself as we enter the third Christian millennium; where do we come from? who are we? and where do we go from here?

Part Three is the 'sharp end' providing a detailed design guide for all aspects of the liturgical space, but

Part Two (identifying the principles behind those guidelines), and Part One (giving the historical and biblical background) provide essential preparation for the task.

These three sections provide a framework suitable for use as three 'terms' of study by a Christian community wishing to undertake a long and careful reappraisal of its communal life in both worship and mission, before drawing up a scheme to alter and improve its buildings to better meet its needs and proclaim its message. For parishes in more of a hurry, a short six week version of the course is provided as a final appendix, suitable for use as a Lent programme for example.

In whatever way the handbook is used, no issue in Church life is more sensitive than that of the nature and character of the place in which the Christian community meets week by week to 'address one another in psalms and spiritual songs, singing and making melody to the Lord' (Ephesians 5.19).

Learning a common language in the design of liturgical space is both an ecumenical and an international movement; it is what the Spirit is saying to the churches, and it is exciting to see. The old game of 'spot the denomination' is becoming increasingly difficult, as we learn to borrow from one another without embarrassment and become a real community once again, with unlocked doors and open windows.

This handbook is designed to enable one another, whatever route has brought us to this point, to approach this issue in a spirit of humility, of open enquiry, and of adventure, so that we may delight in the surprises along the way and be released from past prejudice to be caught up in the exciting enterprise of giving fresh expression, in tangible and visible form, to the truths of the Kingdom of God.

Happy doodling!

PART ONE:
Where do we come from?

Recognising the problem

'Houston, we have a problem'

Commander James Lovell,
Apollo 13 space flight 1972

'What they wish to keep is the expression of the ideals of a small, pietistic society founded by undergraduates at Cambridge at the beginning of the reign of Queen Victoria. So powerful is the influence of faith, even if it be mistaken, and so irresistible is the force of obstinacy.'

Basil Clarke quoted by
Jeremy Haselock, Salisbury
Symposium, 1998.

'In the house he felt he was inside a tethered animal, dumb but feeling. Swallowed by the shouting past.'

E Annie Proulx,
The Shipping News

The village church on the North Cornwall coast was far fuller than I had expected, and it shone with the effects of tender loving care. The congregation contained young as well as old, men as well as women; the liturgy was lively and the interplay between priest and people, revealing both a sense of fun and deep mutual affection, was a delight to see. Here was a model Christian community at worship, a community growing in faith and going places. And yet . . .

One thing troubled me deeply; the building! This adventurous faith community with its evidently gifted priest were struggling to operate in a building which had remained unchanged for the last 100 years. Save for the installation of electric light, the local headquarters for the evangelisation of this part of North Cornwall was visually unchanged from the building as experienced by their forebears who dressed in smocks and long frocks, and who had never seen a tractor, let alone a television. Modern technological humanity, eager to be up to date with every scientific advance and creature comfort, was content, upon engaging in the work of the Christian Community, to use a building which would be condemned as 'unfit for human habitation' in any other walk of life. Surely no organisation that chose to use it as local headquarters could be taken seriously.

'No one today wears clothes, drives cars, or writes journalism like they did a hundred years ago. Why should buildings be any different?'

Richard Rogers, *Sunday Telegraph Magazine* 25 February 1996

*The producers of a recent TV drama set in Edwardian England had to dismantle every sign of modern life when filming in the village street, but inside the village church they didn't have to change a thing.

St John, Worthington, Ohio

'The church may become the place for the enactment of rituals of flower arranging, bell-ringing, cake-baking, hassock-stitching, musical performance and so on, which are in themselves almost unexceptionable yet add up to a massive irrelevance to Christianity, bordering in some cases on being a different religion.'   Robert Maguire, Liturgy North 96

In the parish hall across the yard, an exhibition of local history showed a picture taken in the 1940s of two village children with the working horse of the farm. It was captioned 'Farming Fun' and managed to capture the uncomplicated innocence of those days of short trousers and fairisle pullovers. Those two children were now leading worthies in the life of the village, and had grown up to master the intricacies of modern farming, land-cruisers, mobile phones and all.

What worried me about the church was that, despite the fact that it was evidently trying very hard in its worship, it had not grown up. Its unaltered building spoke more loudly than its energetic priest and spelt out a clear message that the Church was still in short trousers, listening to the wireless and travelling around in a charabanc*. The caption might have read 'Church Fun' – for the building presented a delightful evocation of times past, with very little connection to life as we know it. It provided a harmless pastime for anyone so inclined, but nothing more.

The fossilization of worship spaces is not confined to ancient buildings nor to England. Faith communities in the United States are equally prone to this disease, and the Episcopal Church (perhaps because of its links with the 'Old Country'?) is in imminent danger of drowning in varnish.

The tendency to live with at least one foot in the past is not defined merely by the lack of 'mod cons' – of running hot and cold water, toilets and kitchens and catering facilities – but by the failure to realise that a Christian community at the outset of the third millennium will require a different set of tools from those available 100 years ago if it is to do the work of God in the drastically changed context of a pluralist society.

One of our primary tools is the building which houses the community; the house of the Church. The nature of our society and the critical missionary situation of the Church mean that many different functions are

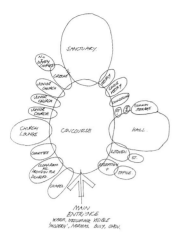

'Bubble' diagram by John Marsh

Care of Churches and Ecclesiastical Jurisdiction Measure 1991

'In Britain we still suffer from a particularly disabling disease that tends to romanticise everything that has lost its purpose – anything that is old.'

Richard Rogers, *Sunday Telegraph Magazine* 25 February 1996

demanded of the same limited floor space. The house of the church is no longer a 'week-end cottage' for busy people to escape to on Sundays; it is a bustling centre of activity for a growing family who are in and out of the place all day, every day of the week.

The Church's building is now called upon to provide within its four walls a home, a worship workshop, a source of inspiration, an oasis of prayer, a community college, an advice centre, a typing pool, a soup kitchen and an operational HQ for a missionary organisation. These multifarious and often conflicting functions require space and flexibility and a new emphasis on quality of provision, to encourage everything to happen that should be happening in our Church's buildings, in terms of both spiritual growth and social action.

Lamentably, comparatively few of our church buildings have yet been refurbished and re-equipped with these needs in mind. Local Christian communities are only now beginning to face up to these new building requirements of a missionary Church, and the temptation to withdraw into a heritage cocoon is very great.

If we consider for a moment the existing stock of English parish churches, the majority of buildings are woefully unsuitable and ill-equipped to serve as 'local centres of worship and mission'.*

Christians are to be found worshipping in long Gothic tunnels, buried beneath heaving seas of pitch pine, cowering beneath balconies and lurking behind pillars. They use on a weekly if not daily basis buildings without running water, and with practically no heat in winter. They attempt to address God in the language of today amidst the debris of yesterday's church and the preservationist constraints imposed by those who have no understanding of the Christian vocation. They are hampered and hindered as no previous Christian generation ever was by the buildings erected to serve them but which now subdue them. If the

Church maintains any desire to proclaim 'release for the captive' it is high time it re-pitched its tents.

Resting content with what previous generations experienced – generations who lived on a different planet as far as understanding of the Church and the world are concerned – reveals five worrying tendencies;

(a) marginalisation; at a time of unceasing change and modernisation in all spheres, when the adaption and refurbishment of outdated buildings is a universal practice, the Church is content to be removed from the mainstream. This vice of stagnation is often dressed up as the virtue of 'creating an oasis of stability in a changing world', but the last dodo said much the same thing.

On a church wedding: 'You've got to keep these old traditions, or we shall lose our culture. It's a bit like Punch and Judy really . . . and it's something to dress up for.'

Raquel, barmaid of the Rover's Return, 'Coronation Street', Granada TV 31 July 1995

(b) eccentricity; because rapid change is the common daily experience of almost every individual in today's world, a false note is struck by any Christian community that eschews change in its own built environment. The honest enquirer would have every reason for treating with suspicion a community so out of step with its surrounding culture that it has become little more than an (occasionally) living exhibit in a folk museum.

'The concept of Christianity is always shaped by the particular concrete form it takes at a period in history. Christianity can become the prisoner of the picture which it has made of itself at a particular time.'

Hans Küng, *Christianity*, p. 7

(c) inconsistency; because every previous generation in the history of the Christian Church has ruthlessly adapted church buildings to suit current theological and liturgical norms, a Christian generation which suddenly ceases to do this is unfaithful to its own tradition. It has thereby abrogated a previously universal pattern of continual evolution.

(d) unfaithfulness; a Christian community which seeks to create an island of no-change in a sea of change – an attitude in which the unaltered building is often the most potent symbol – is unfaithful at the deepest level to the Good News of Jesus Christ, who proclaimed new life through total change – *metanoia*. Such a community despises its own birthright.

(e) spiritualisation; in describing the exciting refurbishment of the chapel and church at St Beuno's Spiritual Exercises Centre, St Asaph, Paul Edwards sj sets the scene by referring to the late Cardinal Heenan's remark that all Jesuit houses tended to have about them an air of 'refined squalor'. This arose from a conviction that there was no time for bothering about mere buildings when there was so much work and prayer to get done.

Jesuit houses are not the only offenders in this respect, for the vast majority of our church buildings could likewise be similarly described as existing in a state of 'refined squalor'. In too many church communities, indifference to the environment of worship is a vice dressed up as a 'spiritual' virtue.

In countless parish churches up and down the land, intelligent men and women, apparently leading otherwise normal lives, are (consciously or not) involved in strange and deeply disturbing practices, perpetuating a religious observance which is marginalised, eccentric, inconsistent, and unfaithful to its own origins. For the first time in history we have a Church which is content to operate out of places of liturgical assembly which contradict, in their layout and design, the Church's own message and theological self-understanding.

We are the first Christian generation which has attempted to separate liturgical design from theology; we proclaim one thing in our preaching and our prayers, and quite another in our weekly polishing of the long-abandoned pulpit. Whereas we tend to say (in a rather spiritually superior way) that the building doesn't matter as long as our heart's in the right place, there can be no doubt that our spiritual ancestors were to be found hacking away at their church building before the ink was dry on the latest theological pamphlet. Current attitudes betray a fatal lack of connection between theology and life; a church fit only for the heritage trail.

Architecture and evangelism are also too easily put asunder, and good evangelists often make poor hosts. Inspired and tireless in their efforts to bring people into the community of faith, they bring their new friends home to a building which has no facilities for hospitality, which is full of unused and antiquated furniture, and which is designed around liturgical set-pieces proclaiming an extinct form of Christianity. Our work to proclaim the living God is thereby undermined and repudiated by buildings which speak of a geriatric God incarcerated in an old folk's home, the kind of rambling Victorian building that real families gave up living in years ago.

'. . . our beloved church buildings . . . are a millstone around our neck so far as the real work of the Church is concerned, for reasons as much or perhaps more to do with our emotional involvement with them as for the often burdensome cost of upkeep.'

Robert Maguire,
Liturgy North 96

Thus the question that needs to be asked is this; 'How do the followers of Jesus of Nazareth today organise themselves in such a way as to make his continued living presence a reality for them and for the world?' To be more precise, 'what are the distinguishing features of the followers of Jesus when they meet as a community, and how can they best use buildings (if they are allowed any) to express their life together and the message they long to share?'

This is the question which this handbook will help us to address as we seek to better understand the relationship between Christian buildings and the message they enshrine and the communities they house; the relationship between dead and living stones.

Reflection: Is there a problem with the church building used by my own worshipping community? What precisely is the trouble with it? Is the problem recognised? Is it being addressed?

2

The roots of our worship

(1) ENCOUNTERING GOD IN THE SACRED PLACE

To better understand what we are doing when we assemble to worship God in a special building set apart for that purpose, and why the building looks like it does, and why it includes particular features common to all such buildings, it is instructive to look back to see how we have arrived at this point.

In the story of the worship of God's people through the ages, a number of significant elements can be discerned which help us to recognise more clearly our roots and origins, which in turn will enrich our on-going relationship with God.

(a) Children of Abraham

If we imagine for a moment that our spiritual ancestry goes back only as far as the sixteenth century, to a time when radical theology smuggled in from Germany happened to coincide with a political impasse between royal and papal spheres of influence, then we would be wrong. We go back much further than that.

'It is belief in the God of Abraham which unites Jews and Christians'
Hans Küng, *Christianity: The Religious Situation of our Time*, p. 41

And if we imagine that we go back to the moment when the Lordship of Jesus the Christ was first proclaimed on these islands, whenever that may have been, we would again be mistaken, for we go back further even than that. Back beyond the sending forth by popes of missionary bishops into the unknown western lands, beyond the regularising by synods of untidy arrangements, beyond the bequeathing of basic building blocks by apostles called to premature and glorious deaths in Rome, beyond the commissioning by the Risen Lord of eleven bewildered men huddled in a barred and bolted room, beyond a passover meal in another room, beyond even the bursting in onto the scene of this man from the margins, Jesus of Nazareth.

For our spiritual ancestry begins with his. Jesus was a Jew, steeped in the scriptures, fiercely proud of his people's special relationship with God, seared by the communal experience of slavery and rescue, of exile and return.

'I insert the Jesus of the Gospels into the geographical and historical realities and into the charismatic religious framework of first-century Judaism, and against this background Jesus the Galilean hasid or holy man begins to take on substance.'
Geza Vermes, Jesus the Jew

'This means that it is not the children of the flesh who are the children of God, but the children of the promise are reckoned as descendants.'
Romans 9.8

To understand him, to follow him, we too must become Jews, in order to grasp fully what it means to enter into our glorious inheritance of 'the children of the promise', i.e. the New Israel, the Church.

'Jesus was a Jew, and his Jewishness unquestionably shaped his mission and ministry . . . Jesus's message and the Christianity that emerged from those who accepted that message can be understood only in the context of the Jewish culture in which they originated.'
Edward Foley, From Age to Age (p. 3)

Edward Foley in From Age to Age, his masterly survey of liturgical development through Christian history, reminds us of a remark of Pope Pius XI that in order to understand his or her faith, 'every Christian needs to become a spiritual Semite'.

Sons and daughters of
Abraham, Huddersfield

Realisation of our descent from Abraham enables us not only to understand Jesus more fully, but also to build unity today with those other children of Abraham, Jew and Muslim, who seek God alongside us from this common starting point. One Christian community that shares a house with Jewish fellow pilgrims is the parish of All Saints, New Albany, Ohio. Hopefully the next book to be written on liturgical design will need to cover inter-faith issues, and it won't be far off.

The real division in our world today is not between one major faith and another, but between those who seek God, by whatever route, and those who deny that there is any search to be made. The more closely we can identify ourselves with our forebears, called upon to recite as their credo 'a wandering Aramean was my father' (Deuteronomy 26.5), the more vivid will be our realisation of just how many there are who walk with us on our journey of faith.

(b) Sacred Stones

'Worship is the basic, fundamental instinct within every creature.'
Michael Marshall
Free to Worship p. 1

The basic instinct of humankind, evidenced in most primitive societies, is to offer sacrifice in order to appease the wrath or procure the favour of a deity. Jewish culture is no exception, as is first shown in the myth of Cain and Abel (symbolising the two rival communities of nomadic herdsmen and sedentary farmers) who each make an offering to the Lord of their respective 'fruit of the ground'.

'In the course of time Cain brought to the Lord an offering of the fruit of the ground, and Abel brought of the firstlings of his flock and of their fat portions.'
Genesis 4.3–4a

Evidently Cain and Abel had not heard Rodgers' and Hammerstein's appeal in 'Oklahoma!' that 'the farmer and the cowman should be friends', and it all ends in tears. It is highly significant, as we shall see, that the nomadic herdsman comes out top, 'And the Lord had regard for Abel and his offering'.

'Then Noah built an altar to the Lord, and took of every clean animal and of every clean bird, and offered burnt offerings on the altar.'
Genesis 8.20

The first thing that Noah does on making a landfall is to build an altar and to make sacrifice, and we are told that this has an immediate desired effect in appeasing the Lord who 'smelled the pleasing odour' and decides to go easier on humankind from now on.

'Then the Lord appeared to Abram and said, "To your descendants I will give this land." So he built there an altar to the Lord, who had appeared to him.'
Genesis 12.7

'Abraham expressed his awareness of Yahweh and his trust in God-with-us by making sacrifice in the only way he knew – in the way his culture had taught him.'

Gerard Pottebaum, *The Rites of People*

As the story related in Genesis edges from myth into history, the patriarchs are seen responding to God's covenant and promise by erecting piles of stones in various places where God has made himself known to them and blessed them. Whether in the joy of thanksgiving, when Abram first receives God's promise at Schechem, or in the darkness of blind obedience, when Abraham prepares to sacrifice his own son, encounters with God bestir in the patriarchs a desire to name and set apart these holy places, and to identify them by the building of an altar of sacrifice. Amidst the terrors of the wild and of the unknown, they carve out places of meaning and particularity where they can commune with the transcendent power of God. They show us what it means to create sacred space, 'a place of regeneration, creativity and transformation'.

Things begin to get a little more regularised and ship-shape when we are given, through the mediation of Moses, some basic rules and regulations for the ordering of the sacred space.

Immediately after receiving the Ten Commandments on Mt Sinai, Moses is told by God that the people, instead of attempting to make idols or images to represent God, must build an altar on which to sacrifice their offerings, the fruit of their labours. Interestingly, the altar is to be made of earth or of rough stones, using God-given materials in their raw state, untouched by man's handiwork.

'An altar of earth you shall make for me and sacrifice on it your burnt offerings and your peace offerings, your sheep and your oxen; in every place where I cause my name to be remembered I will come to you and bless you.
And if you build it of stone, you shall not build it of hewn stones; for if you wield your tool upon it you profane it.'

Exodus 20.24–25

As we shall see, it is highly significant in view of current trends in the design of Christian altars, that the altar which Moses is commanded to build is not to be approached by steps (although for quite different reasons than those cited today!). It is to be of the earth and on the earth, part and parcel of God's provision for his people through the given-ness of creation.

'And you shall not go up by steps to my altar, that your nakedness be not exposed on it.'

Exodus 20.26

There is to be no limitation of time and space in honouring God in this way; an altar may be built 'in every place where I cause my name to be remembered'. There says God, 'I will come to you and bless you'.

Later, the Book of Exodus gives precise instructions (chapters 24 to 31) for the construction of the altar – square in shape and of acacia wood – and for the setting apart, ordination and vesting of a priesthood to serve it. Nothing is left to chance, everything is prescribed in great detail, in the provision for the people of God of a sanctuary, a holy place, as a symbol of God's presence among them; 'Let them make a sanctuary, that I may dwell in their midst' (Exodus 25.8).

'Even the sparrow finds a home, and the swallow a nest for herself, where she may lay her young, at thy altars, O Lord of hosts, my King and my God.'

Psalm 84.3

'The altar . . . a place of terror and shuddering'.

St John Chrysostom

'Primitive people found a clear distinction between so-called sacred and profane space. Sacred space is the place of regeneration, creativity and transformation. Sacred space provides an anchor for one's existence in the midst of the hazards of the environment. This experience of sacred place is all but lost on our contemporary culture.'

Huffman & Stauffer, *Where We Worship*, p. 8

The sanctuary and its altar are at one and the same time a symbol of security and safety at the heart of God's covenant with his people, and a place of encounter with the terrifying unknowable God, a frontier between earth and heaven.

This sanctuary is not however to be some static holy place to which the people of God make pilgrimage. In a tremendously significant revelation which set Judaism apart from all other surrounding religions (and which again is highly relevant to contemporary liturgical thinking), the people of God are set free from dependence on a single dot on the map. Instead of the people of God having to journey to him, God will travel with them, that every place where the sanctuary is set up may become holy ground. The altar is to be made in such a way (Exodus 27.4 and 6) that it may be carried by the people of God on their journey. By means of this sanctuary, God will come to be with his people, wherever they go.

We note how utterly inappropriate it would be for an altar of this kind to be housed within a temple. This altar is a nomad's altar, and should the need for protection from the elements arise, all that would be needed is a tent.

Reflection: Where in my life do I feel most keenly aware of the presence of God? Is it a particular place or a set of criteria which may be met in any number of places?

3

The roots of our worship

(2) ENCOUNTERING GOD ON THE MOVE

(a) Ark

'There I will meet with you, and from above the mercy seat, from between the two cherubim that are upon the ark of the testimony, I will speak with you of all that I will give you in commandment for the people of Israel.'

Exodus 25.22

More important even than the altar however, in the descriptions of the sanctuary provided in Exodus, is the Ark. Details of its construction (Exodus 25.10–22) precede those concerning the altar. Not only will the ark house the very tablets of stone upon which God's sacred law has been written, but God will use the ark as a place of meeting with his people.

'You shall make poles of acacia wood, and overlay them with gold. And you shall put the poles into the rings on the sides of the ark, to carry the ark by them.'

Exodus 25.12–14

As with the altar, so with the ark; instructions are given not only for the making of this holy object itself, but also for the means by which it is to be made portable. Moreover, a tent – the tent of meeting – was to be erected over the ark, to signify that henceforth God would pitch his tent among his people.

'And let them make me a sanctuary, that I may dwell in their midst.'

Exodus 25.8

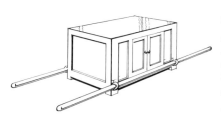

Thus the Jewish religious genius gives a new dimension to the concept of sacred space. There is no shortage of detail; God will indeed come to his people in a particular way in space and time, but we note for future reference that above all it is not a static concept. God will come to his people on the move, wherever they are.

The Jewish people have always been a people deeply conscious of the power of the Word of God, given

eternal expression in the Law ('Torah') handed down through Moses. A glimpse of the dramatic effectiveness of the Law to renew God's people is given in the moving account of the rediscovery of the book of the Law of the Lord in the temple by Hilkiah the high priest during the reign of King Josiah (640–609 BC).

'Then Shaphan the secretary told the king, 'Hilkiah the priest has given me a book.' And Shaphan read it before the king. When the king heard the words of the law he rent his clothes.'

2 Chronicles 34.18–19

The Temple had fallen on hard times during the reigns of his predecessors, and Josiah had set in motion a thoroughgoing repair and maintenance programme for the building. While clearing out the cupboards, Hilkiah the priest stumbled on a dust-covered tome which turned out to be nothing less than 'the book of the law of the Lord given through Moses'.

Shamed by what he has heard, Josiah summons to the temple all the elders of Jerusalem and 'all the people both great and small' for a corporate act of repentance and renewal (verses 29–31).

'The law of the Lord is perfect, reviving the soul; the testimony of the Lord is sure, making wise the simple.'

Psalms 19.7

There is no question here but that the Law could be for the Jewish people not a dead letter, but a life-giving transforming force.

Although later historical events would bring about a total domination of the Law over other elements in the religious life of Israel, we see at the outset a true balance in the provision of the Old Covenant between altar and ark, between the offering of sacrifice and reverent attention to the Law of God written on tablets of stone; between deed and word.

(b) Journey

'It is no coincidence that the first Christians were called followers of the Way. It is still the case that the best metaphor of the Christian life is journey or pilgrimage.'

Stephen Cottrell, Liturgy North 96

We see therefore in Exodus how the primitive concept of holy place is given a new dynamic in the complementary concept of God journeying with his people to meet them wherever they come to rest. Crucial to this understanding is the experience of journey.

'the Lord had regard for Abel and his offering, but for Cain and his offering he had no regard.'

Genesis 4.4–5

Mention has already been made of the violent jealousy that arose between Abel the herdsmen and Cain, the tiller of the ground, when their respective offerings to God were perceived as differing in relative value.

Whereas today we would assume that the Israeli arable farmer growing his citrus fruit for export had a higher social standing than the nomadic herdsman of the semi-arid outback, at the time when the book of Genesis was being written, the reverse was true.

Underlying this elevation of the herdsman over the tiller of the ground in the Cain and Abel story is the high social standing, universal in the Middle East of this period, of those who roamed free with their flocks and herds in contrast to those perceived as grubbing around in the soil to scratch a living.

In that context, a nomadic lifestyle, far from being socially suspect, was a sign of prosperity. Moreover, for the Jewish people it was a lifestyle underlaid not merely by an appropriate agricultural policy but by a deep-seated spiritual tradition, which was both theological and instinctive.

'Now the Lord said to Abram, ''Go from your country, and your kindred and your father's house to the land that I will show you''.'

Genesis 12.1

At the beginning of our story, the very first word that the Lord says to Abram, his chosen instrument, is 'Go'.

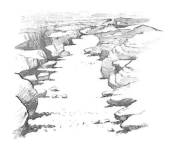

That word 'GO' is seared into the very flesh of Israel, a driving force in its religious consciousness to this very day. They are a people who have had to learn how to remain in the presence and under the blessing of God whilst being always on the move, often amidst appalling hardship.

'By faith Abraham obeyed
when he was called to go
out to a place which he
was to receive as an
inheritance; and he went
out, not knowing where he
was to go. By faith he
sojourned in the land of
promise, as in a foreign
land, living in tents.'

Hebrews 11.8–9

Abram is required to abandon every single known point of reference in his life, every certainty, in order to know God and to receive his blessing. The writer of Hebrews encapsulates Abraham's greatness as the supreme man of faith when he reminds us that 'he went out, not knowing where he was to go.'

Whereas for Western Europeans today, the term 'nomad' conjures up a picture of a Bedouin tribesman, tattered rags blowing in the wind, inhabiting a semi-desert wasteland, the story of Abram who, through his wanderings, became Abraham, confers on the nomadic lifestyle ultimate spiritual legitimacy. For the Jews of this period, the tent, not the palace, is the true measure of authenticity.

'On the day that the
tabernacle was set up, the
cloud covered the
tabernacle, the tent of the
testimony; and at evening
it was over the tabernacle
like the appearance of fire
until morning. So it was
continually; the cloud
covered it by day, and the
appearance of fire by
night. And whenever the
cloud was taken up from
over the tent, after that the
people of Israel set out;
and in the place where the
cloud settled down, there
the people of Israel
encamped.'

Numbers 9.15–17

When we come to a later stage in our story as sons of Abraham, to our communal wilderness experience emerging from slavery and humiliation, we see how continually being 'on the road' is part and parcel of the Jewish perception of faithfulness to God. The tabernacle, 'the tent of the testimony', enclosing ark and altar, was continually moved on as the people of God followed the signs of God's presence. They embraced what we might call a Romany way of life, always on the move, never sure how long they would have in any one place.

'And you shall make
response before the Lord
your God, "A wandering
Aramean was my father;
and he went down into
Egypt and sojourned there,
few in number; and there
he became a nation, great,
mighty and populous".'

Deuteronomy 26.5

In the liturgy of the offering of the First Fruits (Deuteronomy 26.1–11), to be celebrated upon taking possession of the land promised them, the worshipper is to offer at the altar the first fruits of this new country. In his profession of faith before the priest, he is to recite a credo recalling the wonderful works of God in calling, guiding, rescuing and protecting his chosen people. The credo is to begin with the words 'A wandering Aramean was my father', for here in the original journey of Abram going out into the unknown at the command of God lies the true identity of the chosen people of God. Here is the secret of their greatness and their nationhood.

'The Biblical Hebrews belonged to the floating class of semi-nomad. This picture agrees with the description of Abraham as . . . a "sojourner" (ger) in the midst of the established peoples of Canaan. With his flocks and his family he moved through the sparsely settled hill country, wandering from place to place.'

B. W. Anderson, *Living World of the Old Testament*, p. 23

As we shall see, in the later period of the Davidic kings, this great spiritual tradition was threatened by monarchical ambition. The prophet Nathan, in an attempt to recall Israel to its roots, takes the argument an astonishing step further which prefigures the Christian insight of Incarnation. Not only are the people of God to remember always that they were called to the nomadic life; they must realise too that God himself is a nomad, accompanying his people on their wanderings.

'I had not dwelt in a house since the day I brought up the people of Israel from Egypt to this day, but I have been moving about in a tent for my dwelling.'

2 Samuel 7.6

Having this nomadic spiritual tradition in his blood-stream, Jesus himself embraced a peripatetic ministry, in which he had nowhere to lay his head, nowhere to call his own.

'And Jesus said to him, "Foxes have holes, and birds of air have nests; but the Son of man has nowhere to lay his head".'

Matthew 8.20

It is no coincidence that it is when the Christian Church has been most faithful to this tradition that it has known periods of vigorous growth. In its early days as a proscribed sect, when it operated out of borrowed buildings in short bursts of activity pending the next police raid, or when reformers like Francis or Dominic recalled it to the uncertainty of life on the road, or when the church planting movement in our own day recalls us to worship in schools and pubs and hired halls, again and again the experience of re-pitching our tent has reinvigorated the community of faith with a dependence upon the mercy of God and a loving intimacy with him in his power and provision.

Whether we like the idea or not therefore, we must learn as a community of God's people to go in for camping in a big way.

'We through the generations came Here by a way we do not know From the fields of Abraham, And still the road is scarce begun.'

Edwin Muir, *The Succession*

Reflection: Is there any way in which our local Christian community could express, in its worship and lifestyle, the insights of the semi-nomadic way of life?

'Abram called by God to leave home.' Prototype clay model by Rory Young for the new Great West Door, York Minster. Copyright the Dean and Chapter of York Minster.

4

The roots of our worship

(3) FROM TEMPLE TO TABLE

The route from Temple to table takes us through the three main historical influences in Jewish religious experience.

(a) The Temple

Between 1000 BC and AD 100 three pivotal events transformed the Jewish religious tradition out of all recognition.

'Yet his sons did not walk in his ways, but turned aside after gain; they took bribes and perverted justice.'

1 Samuel 8.3

In the eleventh century BC, Israel was growing restless. It was tired of being pushed around by neighbouring kingdoms with more clout than it could muster, and the antics of Samuel's sons as Judges of Israel – with hands in the till as well as on the reins – was the final straw.

The preferred solution to this impasse was a monarchy. Indeed, so desperate were the people to acquire this new status symbol, that they clamoured for a king like children for sweets.

'. . . he will take the tenth of your flocks, and you shall be his slaves. And in that day you will cry out because of your king, whom you have chosen for yourselves; but the Lord will not answer you in that day. But the people refused to listen to the voice of Samuel; and they said, "No! but we will have a king over us".'

1 Samuel 8.17–19

Despite dire warnings from Samuel, the people were adamant; 'No! but we will have a king over us'. The joys of being a theocracy – unique among the nations – had palled; they now simply wanted to be just like everyone else. A classic case of transference from frying pan into fire.

Things began well enough, with three successive kings – Saul, David and Solomon – who were giants among men, and under whom Israel became again a power to be reckoned with. These kings, their deeds and their palaces drew gasps of astonishment from neighbouring royal houses and caused their own people to swell with pride.

At the same time however, it was not long before the monarchy (in the reign of David) sought to give concrete expression to the union of church and state which had made Israel what it was; why not enshrine the ark in a permanent structure, alongside the king's palace, to make the world marvel at the majesty and might of God and of his anointed king?

The tussle between King David and the prophet Nathan on this subject reveals the religious dilemma facing Israel. It seemed a natural progression to build a permanent home for the ark of God now that Israel had 'arrived' not only in the Promised Land, but as an international power to be reckoned with. Yet there was wariness lest they be unfaithful to God's revelation of himself.

In the event, neither the eloquence of Nathan, nor the reported indignation of God himself, were to be any match for a king with a bee in his bonnet.

Ambition won the day and a temple was built, although not until about 922, and not by David, but by Solomon his son. The result was a magnificent edifice, a wonder of the known world. At first *the* place, it very soon became the *only* place in which sacrifice could be made and to which pilgrimage could be undertaken.

Furthermore, by its hierarchy of holy spaces symbolised by the series of courts approaching the holy of holies, the Temple reinforced the rigidly hierarchical system by which man was now to approach God. This hardening of the arteries in the relationship between God and his people was a disease which was to rear its

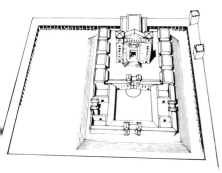

head again in Christianity in its later periods of development, and deeply influence its own architectural understanding of sacred space. Only now is the patient beginning to return to normal.

The building of the Jerusalem Temple was a tremendous feat, but it was apostasy. The Jewish religion thereby was nationalised, centralised and politicised; it became static. The Jews were still the pilgrim people of God, but in an entirely different way. Instead of God living in a tent, he was enshrined in a magnificent temple. Instead of his people encountering God alongside them on the road, they must now take the road to Jerusalem where he was to be found at journey's end. No longer did God pitch his tent among men.

If the dedication of the Temple was a peaceful affair, albeit controversial and life-changing, the next two major events shaping Jewish religious thought and practice, both of which involved the temple, were cataclysmic.

Firstly in 587 BC, the temple was destroyed by the invading Babylonians, who proceeded to carry off the Israelites into captivity in exile. Although the temple was rebuilt after the Exile, and restored to yet greater magnificence around the lifetime of Jesus, the third blow fell when it was finally razed to the ground by the Romans in AD70.

'But if Judaism was a religion of one sanctuary it came to be equally a religion of one book, and this could be disseminated as its place of worship could not.'

A Liturgical Brief, Benedict Green, *Towards a Church Architecture*, p. 93

It was through these dramatic events that the true genius of the Jewish religion revealed itself. Having centralised its sacrificial system, all its eggs had been placed in one basket and all the eggs were smashed. Instead of reverting to the previous pattern of widespread priestly sacrifice in localised sanctuaries, it dispensed with sanctuary and sacrifice altogether; first for a limited period (during the Exile) and then permanently (after AD70).

In an astonishing mutation, Judaism showed its incredible capacity to adapt and survive by going back to its roots and re-expressing its identity as the faith of the pilgrim people of God.

To achieve this remarkable feat, the Jews built upon two foundation stones, one of which had been quarried during the Exile, and one which had been part of their life throughout their journey through history; i.e. the synagogue and the home.

Although this development took place just after the lifetime of Jesus, we can see how the growing Jewish emphasis on public assembly for non-sacrificial worship, and upon the home as the heart of worship, were to become formative influences on the fledgling Christian community.

(Jesus) 'said to him, "see that you say nothing to any one; but go, show yourself to the priest, and offer for your cleansing what Moses commanded, for a proof to the people".'

Mark 1.44

Although Jesus himself acknowledged the priestly system and was happy to continue using the temple as a base for his teaching even after his confrontation with the temple authorities, it is the synagogue and the home (or private room) which predominate in the accounts of his ministry.

(b) The Synagogue

'The original meaning of synagogue was 'gathering' . . . only later did the term come to mean a place, a building.'

Cole and Morgan, *Six Religions in the Twentieth Century*

The synagogue (literally 'gathering') had been developed as an alternative means of maintaining religious identity during the years of the Exile when the Jews were deprived of access to the Temple.

'. . . and he closed the book, and gave it back to the attendant, and sat down; and the eyes of all in the synagogue were fixed on him. And he began to say to them, "Today this scripture has been fulfilled in your hearing".'

Luke 4.20–21

The synagogue thus became the place of regular meeting – on sabbaths and other holy days – to study the Law and to pray. By the time of Jesus, a synagogue was to be found in practically every settlement where Jews lived, and was the scene of some of Jesus' most important proclamations in word and deed of the new relationship with God.

'And they went into
Capernaum; and
immediately on the
sabbath he entered the
synagogue and taught.'

Mark 1.21

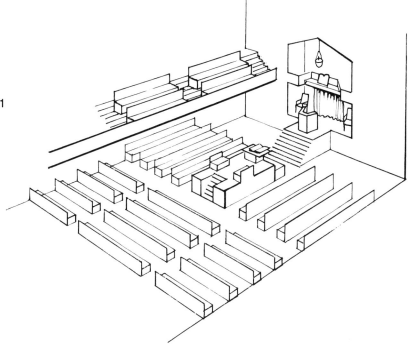

'For several days (Paul)
was with the disciples in
Damascus. And in the
synagogues immediately
he proclaimed Jesus,
saying, "He is the Son of
God".'

Acts 9.20

This well-established pattern of using the given framework of the indigenous religious system was evidently
continued by his first followers. Significantly this
included even Paul, the turncoat Pharisee who, immediately after his sudden conversion, continued to
see the synagogue as his natural habitat.

(c) The Home

'. . . and these words
which I command you this
day shall be upon your
heart; and you shall teach
them diligently to their
children, and shall talk of
them when you sit in your
house . . . and you shall
write them on the
doorposts of your house
and on your gates.'

Deuteronomy 6.6–7 and 9

From the beginning, the home had been the place for
blessing and prayer in Jewish experience, and indeed
some of the early prayer forms, such as the Shema or
'Hear O Israel', had begun life in the home although
later transferred to the synagogue.

Around his own family table in Nazareth, Jesus learnt
to pray and to recall the wonderful works of God, and
for Christians it is the upper rooom which will forever
be associated with his particular modus operandi.

It was the traditional prayers of blessings before and
after festive meals which provided the context in
which Jesus chose to reveal to his closest friends, in a

'The authenticity of the rites which Jesus performed comes from his capacity to recognise the action of God in ordinary events and to give new meaning to ordinary rites which people already identified as their own.'
Gerard Pottebaum, *The Rites of People*

'And no longer shall each man teach his neighbour and teach his brother, saying, "Know the Lord", for they shall all know me, from the least of them to the greatest, says the Lord.'   Jeremiah 31.34

'Thus says the Lord of hosts: In those days ten men from the nations of every tongue shall take hold of the robe of a Jew, saying, "Let us come with you, for we have heard that God is with you".'
Zechariah 8.23

prophetic act using bread and wine, both his imminent fate and the means by which his followers would encounter him again. In these prayers of blessing too, lay the seeds from which later eucharistic prayers would grow. In so doing, he took familiar things and normal customs and invested them with new significance as channels of God's grace.

So it was that Judaism turned catastrophe into long-term advantage, freeing itself from dependence on either a single sacred place (so vulnerable to attack), or an institutionalised sacrificing priesthood. Out of adversity evolved a radically redesigned religious system, no longer a hostage to fortune, but capable of being established anywhere and of mobilising the whole people of God into a community of faith. Judaism was thus re-established as a religion of tent dwellers able to encounter God wherever they happened to find themselves. Furthermore Judaism as a 'spectator sport' was no more; all would be priests and all prophets.

Reflection: What elements in present day practice in our community of faith can we trace back to the experience of Jesus and his first followers in the synagogue and in the home?

5

The First Christians (1)

(A) THE BORROWERS

We have attempted so far to take a look at the concept of sacred space, of places of assembly and of encounter with God, in the light of the earliest pages of our communal story, from the call of Abraham to the death of Jesus.

We can now turn to look at what happened after the lifetime of Jesus. How did his followers first make use of buildings and how did subsequent Christian generations develop the story?

Hopefully we shall then be in a better position to start work on our own 'houses of the church' in order that they may more effectively demonstrate who we are, where we have come from, and where we are going, as God's people on the move.

'For the early Christians, the place of assembly was not as important as the assembly itself.'
Michael Komechak, *Historical Perspective Building & Renovation Kit*, ed Brown

For the first few centuries of the Christian story, the followers of Jesus were like Mary Norton's Borrowers – little people in a big world getting great things done in an unobtrusive way. Like the Borrowers, the first Christians showed great ingenuity in adapting for temporary periods other people's buildings to meet their own needs. They were borrowers and they travelled light.

'The first generation of those who believed in Jesus of Nazareth as the Messiah still remained completely integrated within Judaism'
Hans Kung, *Christianity*, p. 71

To start with, the followers of Jesus simply made use of the buildings of the Jewish religious community of which they still formed part. For a period of several years it remained an open question whether the teachings of Jesus enshrined a Jewish reform movement or contained the seeds of a separate religion altogether.

'And on the sabbath day they went into the synagogue and sat down . . . and the rulers of the synagogue sent to them, saying, "Brethren, if you have any word of exhortation for the people, say it".'

Acts 13.14–15

'and the number of the disciples multiplied greatly in Jerusalem, and a great many of the priests were obedient to the faith.'

Acts 6.7

'They started to teach and preach in the synagogues, but they soon found themselves excluded. So they met wherever it was convenient. Where they were God was, for his name is Immanuel.'

E. A. Sovik, *Architecture for Worship*, p. 13

'For the earliest community, the execution of its leader James and those close to him represented a catastrophe from which it was never to recover'.

Hans Küng, *Christianity: The Religious Situation of our Time*, p. 86

The leaders entrusted with the Good News continued to make their way as usual to the synagogues (Acts 13.14) and to the Temple (Acts 3.1) where they found the professional clergy by no means hostile to their message.

The honeymoon period did not last long. Rapid expansion of this radical new movement, whose adherents came to be known as Christians (i.e. those who proclaimed Jesus as God's Christ, his Anointed), led to a severing of the links with Judaism towards the end of the first century.

According to Küng, the persecutions which led to the deaths of first Stephen, and then James son of Zebedee, had fatal consequences for the relationship of the early Christian community to the Jewish authorities.

There was however, already more to the Christian movement than the Jewish-Christian community in Jerusalem. By the turn of the first century Foley estimates the Christian movement to have numbered around 20,000, growing to around 7 million by AD300 – a significant minority in an empire of 60 million. The increasingly high visibility of the Christian community is attested to by the attention paid to its suppression by a number of emperors, beginning with Nero in AD64.

'It was a time when one could recognise a church: urban, Gentile and Hellenized. Lacking a central government, pluriform in practice and belief, more familial than institutional, the years 100–313 might be called the era of the domestic church'

Edward Foley, *From Age to Age*, p. 27

'We may call it the house-church, because it always combined under one roof both domestic and liturgical spaces. For us the 'house-church' constitutes the primitive tradition, original and theologically sound, in relation to which all subsequent developments, however grandiose their theological, pastoral or artistic structures, will in a sense never be anything more than derivative and secondary.'

Frederick Debuyst, *Jean Cosse: Des Maisons pour Vivre*, p. 98

So the Christians had to go on borrowing places to meet, usually the houses of its more wealthy adherents and, to a lesser extent, the catacombs. This was the era of the domestic church.

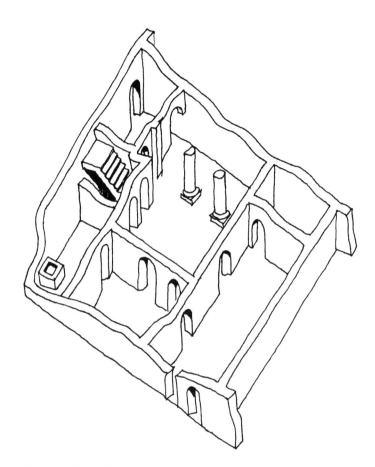

House at Dura Europos

As it is in the natural way of things, some of these temporary arrangements edged into permanency, and houses were gradually commandeered as more or less permanent meeting places for the Christian assembly. Larger houses of this period, consisting of a series of rooms grouped around an open courtyard, made excellent venues for the Christian assembly to meet, providing a progression of spaces suitable for the different elements of the community's life and worship. The earliest example identified to date is the house at Dura Europos in Syria.

'The extraordinarily rapid growth of Christianity had certainly found an adequate instrument, totally flexible, in this 'place' at once domestic, liturgical and evangelistic . . . a place embodying an almost unbelievable innovation, radically different from the temple of the pagans and of the Jews.'

Debuyst Jean Cosse: *Des maisons pour Vivre* p. 98

'As the communities grew and became richer, they acquired houses for their permanent use.'

Peter Cobb, 'The Architectural Setting of the Liturgy', *The Study of Liturgy*, Ed. Jones, p. 474

'Come to him, to that living stone, rejected by men but in God's sight chosen and precious; and like living stones be yourselves built into a spiritual house.'

1 Peter 2.4–5

Built about the year AD200 and converted into a church around AD232, two rooms were knocked into one to form a suitable place (approx 16 ft × 55 ft/ 5m × 17m) for the community's eucharist, while a smaller room was set aside for Christian initiation, as indicated by frescoes relating to baptism. In other cases, the atrium, with its pool or fountain, would have made an appropriate setting for baptism. Nearer to home, although a little later in the 4th century, the Roman villa at Lullingstone was reoccupied and adapted for Christian worship.

The use of the catacombs – subterranean burial chambers existing in many cities of the empire – as places for regular worship, was much less widespread than our romantic notions of the early Church might lead us to suppose. Firstly they were too restricted in space for Christian assembly, and secondly the persecutions that drove the Church underground were far too sporadic to have had a lasting effect on Christian architecture. The lasting effect of the catacombs was to be seen in another area, that of the cult of the martyrs, which would influence both worship and architecture for centuries to come.

The Christian community in this domestic period of its development was content to borrow, to travel light, because of its conviction that the only construction work they were called to do was that of building a community of living stones.

'It is not a place that is called 'church', nor a house made of stones and earth . . . What then is the church? It is the holy assembly of those who live in righteousness.'

Clement of Alexandria
(Strom 7.5)

'There is no peculiarly Christian type of architecture because Christian worship does not centre on a cult object or require a fixed altar which have to be housed in a special way'

Peter Cobb, *Study of Liturgy*,
p. 473

'Here Constantine was neither a pious Christian nor a hypocrite. rather, he was a statesman who coolly took Christianity into the calculations of his power politics.'

Hans Küng, *Christianity: The Religious Situation of our Time*, p. 177

'but for better or worse the deed was done: after nearly three centuries of outlaw status, Christianity was "official".'

James Bulloch, *Pilate to Constantine*

As late as the third century, Minicius Felix was still able to proclaim 'We have no temples; we have no altars', for the static and hierarchical notions of temple religion had not yet begun to wrap its tentacles around the youthful Church.

The community carried no baggage, was free from the burden of possessions, and for these reasons was able to move quickly and effectively as it quietly turned the world upside down.

(B) THE ADAPTORS

In 313 the Christian Church was made an offer it couldn't refuse, for in that year Constantine became the first emperor astute enough to realise that if an empire as unwieldy and as troublesome as his, was going to be held together, it was better to have those apparently indestructible Christians on his side.

The fact that Constantine then waited a further 24 years before finally submitting to baptism a few weeks before his death makes the sincerity of his 'conversion' extremely doubtful. The eventual convergence of a proud but nervous State and a confident but vulnerable Church was, however, inevitable.

It is not difficult to imagine the pressure on the leaders of the Church, emerging from the darkness of persecution, to go along with some form of concordat with the State. What could be more important than establishing legitimacy and winning freedom to proclaim the life-giving message of Jesus Christ to the ends of the earth? The repercussions of their decision would have been impossible to foresee.

It was not long however, before the Church received the invoice for the price to be paid. Within a few years, an unbaptised emperor was calling Church Councils, intervening in doctrinal disputes concerning the nature of Christ, while at the same time status and privilege began to eat away at the Church's soul, seducing its leaders into displays of the trappings of imperial power, into plotting and intrigue. In a short time, baptism ceased to be a costly process by which (mainly adult) converts crossed over into a new world of the tightly-knit Christian community, and became instead a familiar social occasion. Christian allegiance became by and large a matter of accident of birth rather than of adult conversion.

It was natural that the burgeoning Christian Church should seek new premises for its assemblies; it was time to 'go public'. Indeed it was necessary that it should do so, for the domestic places of assembly could no longer accommodate the greatly increased numbers.

They gave rise to some fascinating questions for the Christian Church. Its complete newness as an official organisation meant that it had no architectural tradition of its own; it was coming out into the open without a stitch of clothing. Naked in the market place, it must look around and find a new suit from somewhere, and quickly.

What building form would it be most appropriate for the Church to adopt? Were there any buildings around which the Church could, with minimal adaptation, use for its gatherings while it worked out a permanent solution? What kind of building did the Church feel most drawn to as a model for its own building programme in the future?

The Church's choice is highly significant, for it chose neither temple nor synagogue nor house as its model, but the *basilica*, or hall of the king. From the outset, the Church thereby aligned itself with secular authority

'The expansion of the church and its growing status in society brought with them the external trappings of imperial favour. Bishops were granted various honours and wore the insignia of civil magistrates.'

Edward Foley,
From Age to Age, p. 43

'Christianity under Constantine had to find a new architecture of a higher order, public in character, resplendent in material and spacious in layout.'

R. Krautheimer, *Early Christian and Byzantine Architecture*, p. 19

'The basic picture, implied or explicit, is of God the Almighty King – and, since Constantine, of God the Almighty Emperor.'

David Jenkins, *God, Miracle and the Church of England*

'Consequently, the table, like the fountain, lies in the middle in order that the flocks may surround the fountain.

John Chrysostom, *Second Baptismal Instruction*

'Except in the basilicas erected to the memory of some martyr, the altar had no fixed place, and the same must be said of the ambo. Both were generally close to the assembly, inside the nave.'

Frederic Debuyst, *Modern Architecture & Christian Celebration*, p. 24

in an extremely high profile manner. The basilica was an imposing civic building redolent with the power and the glory of the Roman Empire. The type of building previously associated in every town with the dispensation of law and order now became synonymous with Christian assembly. This was to have theological as well as liturgical repercussions.

Traditionally a rectangular building with an apse at both ends, the basilica was modified by the Christians who placed an apse at the east end only, in which was placed the bishop's seat with benches at either side for his presbyters. The altar, at first a freestanding wooden structure, stood in front of the apse and not necessarily in a fixed position, enabling the people to gather around it.

Typical layout of early Christian basilica

The ambo or reading desk, stood in the middle of the assembly, while the font was housed in a separate baptistry. Both the proclamation of the word and the initiation of new Christians were emphasized and dignified by being allocated distinctive liturgical spaces of their own.

'The Christian basilica was a great forum for God's people arranged in the hierarchical order espoused by the Roman mentality.'

Michael Komechak, *Historical Perspective Building and Renovation Kit*, ed. Brown

'The Christian basilica, both in function and design, was a new creation within an accustomed framework'.

Richard Krautheimer quoted by Edward Foley in *From Age to Age*, p. 46

'We should not imagine the basilica as forming a complete "church" all by itself. It still remained inside a certain interrelated complex of other Christian buildings: the lodgings of the bishop and his priests, the "class rooms" of the catechumens etc. Well sheltered from the uproar of the street, it was essentially an interior, i.e. the exact opposite of a temple.'

Frederic Debuyst, *Modern Architecture & Christian Celebration*, p. 25

'In one word, the church remained a house into which the basilica had intruded.'

J. Lassus, *Sanctuaires chrétiens de Syrie*, p. 23

The longitudinal plan of the basilica accommodated very well the increasing need for the liturgical processions which expressed so well the imperial character of worship in a Church which had become the handmaid of a mighty empire.

Thus did the Christians, adapting rapidly and skilfully to their new-found status in the world, take to themselves a structure familiar to them from their surrounding culture, and imbue it with theological significance.

But it was not a total capitulation to the ways of the world. In a prefiguration of the modern church complex, the basilica remained but one element in a group of buildings pertaining to the local Christian community. The basilican meeting hall was not yet a monument, but still met Debuyst's criteria defining the true purpose of a house of the Church, i.e. 'to offer to the local community a practicable and hospitable celebration room'.

Reflection: If the Church today was deprived of all its existing buildings, what kind of secular building would it be most appropriate to adapt or to copy to provide places of Christian assembly?

St Paul's, London

6

The First Christians (2)

'Vitruvius recounts the invention of the first building not as revelation but as a gradual process of trial and error involving many, many builders, in which good ideas survived through imitation while bad ones fell by the wayside.'

Pollan, *A Place of my Own*

THE DEVELOPERS

Coming in from the cold, and experiencing sustained and phenomenal growth, the Christian community now walked the corridors of power. As far as buildings went, other people's cast-offs were just not good enough; it was time that the Christian Church bought some new clothes of its own.

As the Christian Church grew and developed, we see how building form was a response to both liturgical need and theological development. Having provided concrete expression of these ideas, Christian buildings themselves provided a catechetical service in stone.

Three purposes can be seen at work:

(i) Ennoblement
As the Church grew in stature and influence, there was a desire to give greater dignity to its buildings.

While the basilican plan prospered in the West, in the Eastern half of the Empire (centred on Constantinople) a central plan, more square than rectangle, was favoured. The magnificent domes which covered them gave to these interiors an open spaciousness and verticality very different from those of the West, where arcades made for sub-divided interiors with greater horizontality of emphasis.

These two building forms, although not in water-tight compartments (domes were sometimes added to basilicas in the West), indicated different instinctive approaches to liturgy arising from different emphases on the nature of the Christian assembly. The East retained a more communal understanding of the Christian community at worship, while the West developed faster a hierarchical understanding.

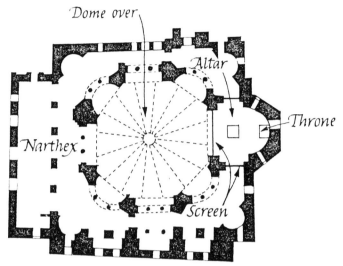

Eighth century orthodox church (Cobb, *Study of Liturgy*, p. 484)

Greater dignity also came to be given to significant objects within the liturgical space, especially where, by so doing, the Church could spell out in concrete form shifts in liturgical and theological emphasis. The ennoblement of the altar for example, gave clear signals about the gradual shift from a communal to a sacrificial understanding of the eucharistic meal.

(ii) Compartmentalisation
The sociological process by which the Church, after Constantine, ceased to be a community of equal commitment and required a professional clergy to keep the show on the road, was soon reflected in the internal layout of its buildings.

Although from the outset the bishop and presbyters seem to have been given reserved seats in the apse, only later did there develop clear demarcation of areas denoting separate ministries, thereby detracting from the essential unity of the Christian assembly.

'The sense of space and the upward 'pull' of the dome, accentuated by its elaborate mosaic decoration, usually culminating in the figure of the Pantocrator at the top, gave a completely different feel to such a building from that in a Western basilica with its strong emphasis on the horizontal perspective. It undoubtedly contributed to the survival of a more corporate sense of the People of God in the East whereas Western architecture emphasised its hierarchical nature.'
Cobb, *Study of Liturgy*, p. 476

'The typical expression of this change was the new location of the altar at the back of the apse, i.e. at the former place of the celebrant's chair.'
Frederic Debuyst, *Modern Architecture & Christian Celebration*, p. 25

'The Christian basilica . . . must be considered as a great, hieratically arranged hall, with one part reserved for the presidency, the other for the body of the faithful.'
Frederic Debuyst, *Modern Architecture & Christian Celebration*, p. 24

The practice of the Church of Scotland in using 'sanctuary' to denote the whole of the worship space, not just a fenced off area within it, is a healthy reminder that New Testament priesthood is exercised by the whole community, not just by a caste within it.

The altar was moved away from the people into the apse (which then came to be ennobled with the name "sanctuary"), dignified with a ciborium (canopy), and 'protected' by low walls. Wooden altars were replaced by ones in stone, often massive in size. The central area of liturgical activity within the nave was also demarcated by low walls, to reserve an area for the reading of scripture and for the ceremonies surrounding the entry and exit of the bishop, now a civic dignitary as well as shepherd of the flock.

Gregory the Great (d. 604) accelerated these tendencies when he raised the floor of the apse in Old St Peter's in Rome, so that the altar could be reconstructed directly above the tomb of S. Peter, and moved the ambo into the sanctuary at the same time.* Thereafter sharp vertical distinction between sanctuary and nave became the norm (and remained so until

*Gregory the Great's unfortunate little re-ordering scheme also had the effect of giving yet greater emphasis to the primitive Christian cult of the martyrs. This led in time to a brisk trade in martyrs' relics, and in turn (towards the end of the first millennium) to the multiplication of altars to house them. Such multiplication – which would have been incomprehensible to the early Church – was further reinforced by the demand for masses for the dead or for the fulfilment of penance, as the Church became less and less a community and more and more a congregation serviced by a priestly caste.

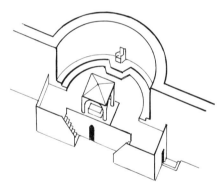

St Peter's, Rome, *c.* 600

the present century), as did the grouping together in the sanctuary of all liturgical furniture (except for the font), thus distancing the people even further from the centre of liturgical action. This latter move reflected the increasing clericalisation of ministry, as liturgical functions formerly exercised by a variety of ministers were vested in a lone priest-presider, who needed everything to hand in the sanctuary, which became the privileged domain of the clergy.

Gradually it became impossible to see the liturgical wood for the trees, and the communal aspects of the eucharistic action were submerged beneath the private and individual. In due course it even came to appear normal for private masses to be said at private altars in private chapels. It is only a short step down the centuries from high medievalism to the innocent-looking but theologically devastating 8 o'clock Communion or early Mass.

(iii) Instruction

Before the days of multi-media communication, the Church's buildings provided an invaluable visual aid by which the Church might address the world and instruct its faithful.

The very shape of the church, its outline in plan form, could provide a useful reminder of the Christian message. For this reason, transepts were added to many Western basilicas, thereby producing a ground plan in the form of the cross and clearly distinguishing a Christian basilica from its imperial progenitor. The repercussions of this tradition can be seen today in many medieval churches in England, where the chancel is deliberately set askew the nave, in order to represent the head of Christ on the cross, leaning to one side.

The sub-divided interiors of the West, as compared with the spacious open interiors of the East, reinforced a developing ecclesiology in which order and hierarchy were becoming of utmost importance. The creation of the sanctuary was designed to instruct the faithful that the eucharist was not so much a communal meal as a holy sacrifice conducted by a consecrated priesthood operating at a different level from the laity. The difference in theological level was rammed home with steps and sealed off with screens. As the ordained priest disappeared into the sanctuary to stand with his back to the people, all pretence of a community in dialogue was abandoned. The enabler became the disabler.

The screened sanctuary has appeared (Middle Ages), disappeared (Reformation), reappeared (Catholic Re-

'The priest progressively took for himself the parts of the liturgy which were normally reserved for the assembly, hindering and finally stopping the direct participation of the faithful.'

Frederic Debuyst, *Modern Architecture & Christian Celebration*, p. 26

vival) and disappeared again (Liturgical Movement) as the Church has looped the loop in liturgical expression of its theological self-understanding.

Until the Reformation however, we can discern a steady and unswerving liturgical development, clearly expressed in building forms, towards separation of function, clericalisation, exclusion of the laity and confusion as to the nature of the Church as assembly of the consecrated people of God.

Post-Reformation polarisation eventually led to the building, not of houses for the people of God, but of throne rooms for the shrivelled fruits of division and separation, i.e. shrines for either the Host or the Book.

Both of these idols – like sex in contemporary culture – were travesties of that which they were intended to signify and enrich. At both ends of the spectrum, the faithful laity were the losers, deprived of Holy Communion and reduced to a rump of that holy priestly people to which God had called them and from which they had been expelled by a politicised ecclesiastical leadership.

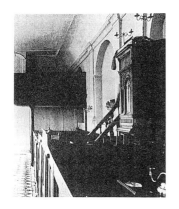

The chancel screen, altar rails and choir stalls typical of the English parish church are but the eventual working-out, in an Anglican context, of these tendencies towards hierarchical separation and restrictive practices.

In these ways did the Christian Church over the first millennium move from 'house' to 'palace', from poverty to privilege, echoing precisely the Jewish movement from tent to temple between Abraham and Solomon.

This was no doubt an inevitable process, but through it the concept of the Christian assembly as the holy priestly people of God was lost, so much so that the word 'church' itself became devalued. No longer designating the assembly, it came to mean merely the building where the assembly met, or at best the sacred institution, distant and magisterial, which controlled those buildings and guarded the holy mysteries celebrated in them. The people of God had forgotten that they were the Church; they merely went to church, to rituals at which they were fast becoming voiceless spectators. The tent was rotting away in the attic.

Reflection: In what ways have our instincts to ennoble and to demarcate our church buildings in our own generation, detracted from their effectiveness as places of Christian assembly for the whole priestly people of God, and as a sign for others of a new kind of society in which the first shall be last?

7

Should Christian Communities have buildings at all?

In the light of our quick dash through the early centuries of Christian development, it is necessary, before going any further, to ask the vital question whether it is legitimate for the Christian community to possess any buildings at all.

Did the Christians of the first centuries take a wrong turning when they began to acquire buildings of their own? By so doing did they abandon the radical insights of Jesus himself? Or does the Church's subsequent consuming interest in the built environment represent simply an inevitable evolutionary process?

Whatever the rights and wrongs of Christian history with regard to buildings, is it justifiable for the Church today, facing decline if not extinction in many areas of the West, to spend so much of its time and resources on maintenance and preservation? How can we get the balance right between idolatry and iconoclasm?

We look in vain to the New Testament for a detailed buildings policy, for the main thrust of its teaching lies in relationships and attitudes, rather than bricks and mortar. Indeed, if we restrict ourselves to the recorded words of Jesus himself (especially if we stay with Mark, the earliest Gospel), it is far from clear that he ever intended to found a separate ecclesial organisation, let alone provide a design bulletin on the buildings appropriate to such a body.

St Peter's, Rome

'And he came to Nazareth, where he had been brought up; and he went to the synagogue, as his custom was, on the sabbath day. And he stood up to read.'

Luke 4.16

'Day after day I was with you in the Temple teaching'

Mark 14.49

'And he taught, and said to them, "Is it not written 'My house shall be called a house of prayer for all the nations.' But you have made it a den of robbers."'

Mark 11.17

'And as he came out of the temple, one of his disciples said to him, "Look, Teacher, what wonderful buildings!" And Jesus said to him, "Do you see these great buildings? There will not be left here one stone upon another, that will not be thrown down.'

Mark 13.2

Jesus certainly made frequent use of the religious buildings of his day, worshipping and expounding the Scriptures in his local synagogue and using the Jerusalem Temple as a base for an intensive period of teaching in the very last week of his life.

On the other hand, Jesus is portrayed as having an ambivalent attitude to sacred buildings. Certainly his only recorded outburst of rage brimming over into violent action is reserved for those he found desecrating the Temple precincts with their cash registers, and yet on the occasion when the disciples (country boys all) threatened to become a little over-excited by the sights of the big city, gasping in wonder at the magnificence of the Temple, Jesus brings them down to earth with a bump, warning them that the Temple's days were numbered. Although far from being an iconoclast, it appears Jesus had an open mind on the significance of sacred buildings; he could take them or leave them. This is entirely consistent with his overriding message that humanity must escape from enslavement to outward forms and external observance, to encounter again the living God within us.

'And day by day, attending the temple together and breaking bread in their homes, they partook of food with glad and generous hearts, praising God and having favour with all the people.'

Acts 2.46–7

When we turn to New Testament writings outside the Gospels, we find that in the period immediately following the death of Jesus, his followers in Jerusalem continued to use, as a matter of course, the familiar pattern of Jewish worship, centred on the Temple and the home. For those living further afield, no doubt the same pattern would have continued in synagogue and home.

As the new wine of Jesus' teaching proved increasingly difficult to contain within the old wine-skin of Jewish religious observance, and as the irrepressible Paul began to mesmerise the Jerusalem Christian Council with his vision of an international corporation to carry the good news to the corners of the known world, things were bound to change.

The followers of Jesus, now a rapidly growing community consisting of groups centred on the major cities of the eastern Mediterranean, found it increasingly inappropriate to go on using Jewish sacred buildings. Such practice was unacceptable in places where the Christian community consisted of non-Jews as well as Jews, but even where the Christian congregation was wholly Jewish, the religious authorities would not have been exactly over the moon about sharing their buildings with a group whose obsession with a failed messiah made their loyalty to the ancient faith extremely questionable.

'Aquila and Prisca, together with the church in their house, send you hearty greetings in the Lord.'

1 Corinthians 16.19

'One who heard us was a woman named Lydia, a seller of purple goods . . . she besought us, saying, "If you have judged me to be faithful to the Lord, come to my house and stay." And she prevailed upon us.'

Acts 16.14–15

As a result the Christians took more and more to meeting in their homes, especially the larger houses belonging to the more wealthy among the converts. Mention is made several times of the 'church' as a congregation meeting in a particular house, and it cannot have escaped the apostles' attention just how convenient it was when someone of means was converted to the new way, thereby easing the problems of arranging Sunday worship. Such a case was Lydia of Philippi, evidently a prosperous businesswoman with her own household, whose immediate response following baptism was to invite Paul and his entourage to stay at her house.

'That is why, for about three centuries, the first generations of Christians were proud of the fact that they had no churches or altars – one of the reasons why the pagans called them 'atheists' or godless people.'

Schillebeeckx, *God the Future of Man*

During this same crucial period of ecclesial formation, while the practical advantages of travelling light as far as sacred buildings were concerned were increasingly apparent, the Christian body was developing the theological system to sustain this instinctive approach. The writer of the Epistle to the Hebrews, for example, provides a comprehensive re-statement of such concepts as 'temple', 'sanctuary', 'sacrifice' and 'priesthood' radically redefined in terms of Jesus' own ministry and sacrificial death. In other words, in the new Christian dispensation, there is no longer any need for sanctuary, altar, sacrifice or human priesthood, nor for a temple to house them. All these have been rendered obsolete by the role of Jesus, the Exalted One, and the concept of temple transposed from dead to living stones. Our home is 'the greater and more perfect tent (not made with hands, that is, not of this creation)' Hebrews 9.11.

'Do you not know that you are God's temple and that God's Spirit dwells in you?'

1 Corinthians 3.16

As the Ohio-based liturgist, Gerard Pottebaum, beautifully describes it, 'We come to realise an even greater discovery that is the joy of our lives: that we ourselves are a tangible expression of the Holy Spirit. That is something to parade through town about . . . and sometimes to enjoy with quiet restraint in a simpler style by touching drinks with a few close friends and offering a toast, together, to life.'

'After Constantine, there was an amazing return to the Old Testament, even down to liturgical texts, ceremonial, priestly clothing and the shaping of the house of God. Everywhere people resorted to the symbolism of a Temple and a Temple liturgy which Jesus himself had relativised and early Gentile Christianity had ignored.'

Hans Küng, *Christianity: The Religious Situations of our Time*, p. 211

Subsequent history has shown that, whether because Christians are very hard of hearing, or because at some crucial period Hebrews was out of print, or simply because it was recognised that we are poor weak creatures unable to exist for long without some form of sacerdotal structure, it took only a few centuries for the Christian Church to effect a volte-face on the issue. As a result of a process discernable from the time of Paul but speeded up dramatically by the concordat with the Roman Empire in AD313, the Church which had begun life as a loose association of messianic Jews transformed itself into a fully fledged relilgous institution complete with its own system of holy places and sacred rituals, together with a consecrated priestly caste to 'do the business for us'.

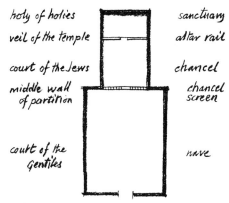

From Patrick Brock, 'A Theology of Church Design'

'In the liturgy (which became now an openly public act) this vision of things provoked a strong emphasis on the presidential function. It was not only in his actual teaching or in the consecration of the eucharist that the bishop presided over the assembly. He appeared more and more to be the viceregens, the living image of Christ in his own person.'

Frederic Debuyst, *Modern Architecture & Christian Celebration*, p. 24

From then on it was only a matter of time before all Christian traditions, no matter how strong their initial reservations, would find themselves drawn irresistibly towards the cherishing of buildings which symbolised their corporate life and which provided a special set-apart place of encounter with the living God, a permanent sanctuary in which the unknowable could be made known.

This is a perfectly understandable development, and one which feeds on a basic human need for safe nests and deep burrows amidst the 'changes and chances of this fleeting world'. Certainly the need not only to use but to possess buildings is a passion among Christians which reformers down the centuries have found themselves powerless to hold in check. No matter how radical or purist the intentions of the founders, nor how determined they are to stand firm, all movements to recall Christianity to its basic origins – whether the 13th century Franciscan reform or the 20th century house-church movement – fall victim sooner or later to this irrepressible urge to possess a holy place of one's own.

What Loisy said of ritual applies equally to the buildings housing the ritual: 'Christianity as a religion needed a ritual . . . the speed with which it was established demonstrates clearly that it was responding to an intimate and inevitable necessity.'

Marvin O'Connell
Critics on Trial p. 248

It may start off innocently enough, a question of convenience unsullied by notions of sacred space, but before very long all Christian groups, whatever

*As a small protest against the abuse of the word church to describe merely the building in which the church meets, I have tried throughout this book to avoid the practice. The correct term the 'house of the church' can be a bit of a mouthful, so sometimes church building or simply building is used instead. It is of course extremely difficult to break free from the bad habits of a Church's lifetime, but every Christian who resolves to do so will be helping to reinvest the word church with its true dignity, and the community it describes with a true sense of its own being and vocation.

'But can one still have any confidence in the Christian cause? Confronted with the third millennium, mustn't one despair of Christianity? Hasn't Christianity become completely incredible and incomprehensible, at least in its European heartlands?

Hans Küng, *Christianity: The Religious Situation of our Time*, p. xx

theological language they may use to articulate what is happening, will find themselves caught up in a process whereby the building comes to symbolise their life and identify their allegiance. To the eternal detriment of the Christian cause and Christian self-understanding, 'Church' is narrowed down to 'church'.* The building comes to attain greater significance than the people who use it and the activities they carry on within it; man seems to want to enslave himself to sabbath after all.

And yet if the Christian Church has indeed been disobedient in littering the face of the earth with so many sanctuaries, it has been *gloriously* disobedient, erecting in every corner of the world countless buildings, all of which have a special character all their own, most of which enable their users to glimpse the glory of the Kingdom, and many of which bring people to their knees in wonder and thanksgiving to God.

All these buildings are ours, and except for a few (built in just the wrong place with pin-point accuracy), they are not going to go away. We have indeed a rich heritage, the potential of which we must maximise for the Kingdom of God. This inherited *embarrassment de richesses* must be held in tension with our Christian calling to travel light as the nomadic people of God, rolling up our tent in readiness for the journey to the next place where God wants us to be. We should not complain; we have only ourselves to blame for the impasse, and the problem is one which serves to remind us how fascinating and exciting it is to be a Christian at this moment in history.

Attempting to be faithful simultaneously to Scripture, to early Christian tradition, and to the given-ness in time and place of our own situation 2000 years down the line, the Christian Church today faces a seemingly impossible task. If however we stop in our ceaseless activity to listen afresh to what the Spirit is saying to the churches, we may hear his voice telling us to enjoy all that we are and all that we have (buildings included) but to do so with a new detachment appropriate to a Church facing unparalleled difficulties in the Western world. In this way we, like the paralytic told by Jesus to take up his bed and walk, will be released from all that paralyses us as a living community of Jesus' disciples, and be freed to take up our tent and re-pitch it wherever and in whatever way we are led.

Reflection: Is my church community's building a help or a hindrance –
(a) in my own growth to spiritual maturity?
(b) in our community's worship?
(c) in our facilitating our community's growth and development?

8

Re-ordering as a priority in a missionary church

'It could well be that we have emotional attachments to our churches as a spiritual affliction, and that this is one of the things standing in the way of the Church's growth in our country.'

Robert Maguire
Liturgy North 96

'Confronted by the new, the Churches have habitually opted for the familiar and safe.'

Pattison, *Art, Modernity and Faith*

'Indifference to art is the most serious sign of decay in any institution'.

Susan Langer, *Feeling and Form*, p. 403

The reasons for *not* re-ordering an existing building are numerous and varied, and the status quo is quite capable of looking after itself without any help from anyone. Just in case, however, there is always a vociferous minority on hand to appeal to the innate fear of change endemic to any social grouping on a downward rather than an upward spiral, where 'consolidation' and 'growth in depth' are spoken of more frequently than 'exploration' and numerical growth.

Alternatively, a community thoroughly committed to change and growth may consider that the re-ordering of its building is of relative unimportance beside the urgent priorities of evangelisation and spiritual formation. Questions of physical environment, of art and design may be relegated to a minor role in strategic planning, on the grounds that it pertains to the material rather than the spiritual sphere.

In this, Puritanism if not Manichaeism lingers on, subverting the Christian vision of the essential unity of creation and of body, mind and spirit, echoing the eternal unity of God himself, Father, Son and Spirit.

Alternatively, Third World priorities are trotted out, not through any genuine concern for the poor, but as a smokescreen to cover inaction. Such objections have apostolic authority (Matthew 26.9) but of a kind that must still bring blushes to the Twelve.

The choice between re-ordering a church building and feeding the poor is like the choice between sunshine

St Augustine, Bradford

'When our church buildings, by their internal layout, stand in the way of the development of the local Church's worship, or the proclamation of the Gospel . . . then the Church has a responsibility before God to seek to change that arrangement.'

Robert Maguire
Liturgy North 96

and rain; we need both. The American liturgist David Philippart reminds us that the poor need beauty as well as food, and points out that the church building is the last truly public place in which beauty may be appreciated. The Church has for most of its history proclaimed God through the expressive arts, and this is no time to be abdicating that role, allowing the city art gallery or the shopping mall to usurp its honoured place.

Even when a community has come to the point of knowing that a re-ordering scheme is long overdue, years may elapse before anything happens. Astonishingly, clergy receive no training in the management of change (probably the most important area of leadership), and understandably may hesitate before subjecting the flock to the upheaval, disruption and pain of a re-ordering project.

Because it can often require only a small group of objectors with sufficient persistence and bile to derail a re-ordering project, the leadership can soon become discouraged. The green pastures of theological college or seminary are no preparation for the sheer nastiness that can be brought to light the moment there is talk of relocating the tabernacle or removing someone's favourite pew (usually the back row). In extreme cases, beleaguered reactionaries will admit to a preference for closure of the building, rather than see one stick or stone tampered with. By comparison, converting the whole congregation to Zoroastrianism would be a piece of cake. But remember, faint heart never won fair Lady Chapel!

In the face of all this potential aggravation, why should we persist in seeing the re-ordering of our place of worship as a gospel imperative today?

There are two main reasons, both concerned with the influence of environment –

1. What buildings say TO us:

Environment – the physical shape and form of those elements which together give us a sense of 'place' – is one of the powerful influences which shape our attitudes and our lives.

Each year governments and local authorities of the Western world, irrespective of political hue, pour enormous resources into renewing the decayed environment of our cities. They do this, not necessarily because they are passionately concerned about townscape, but because they are quite pragmatic in their conviction that refurbished buildings are not unconnected with refurbished lives. Experience has convinced even hard-headed politicians that urban renewal can be the key not just to a lower crime rate, but to a renewed awareness of belonging to a community, a reawakened appreciation of a sense of place.

'Britain's 2,000 worst housing estates can be saved from a downward spiral of poverty and lawlessness by introducing a radical 20-year strategy handing power back to tenants. The Joseph Rowntree Foundation . . . has funded a £1.5m research programme in over 100 estates over the past two years.

'Halton Moor, in Leeds, famous for joyriding, is halfway through renovations of its 1,100 properties; and Meadowell, in North Shields, the scene of riots, has a new youth centre built by a co-operative formed by local young people'.

Independent 6 December 1995

'The planning enterprise is seen to be very much more than mere development control or the production of new schemes of traffic management. It is, in effect, a crusade to end the long blight that has descended upon the City and its region, and to create a modern and thrusting economy . . . Together with the new economy is to come a new society.'

Jon Gower Davies, *The Evangelistic Bureaucrat*, p. 1

Pembroke Street, Plymouth, winner of the 1996 British Urban Regeneration best practice award.
Photo: Planning Week

'It needs to be realised that the architecture of the building is capable of exercising a profound influence on the worshipping community's understanding of itself and its mission.'

Peter Hammond, *Towards a Church Architecture*, p. 32

When it comes to making consumer choices, we are greatly influenced by what buildings say to us. Which shop we go into, which pub we have lunch at, which guest house we stay at, will all be determined to a large extent by the condition and presentation of the building concerned. Not everyone may share my own violent allergy to fluorescent strip lighting, but each of us will have our own indices of those factors which tend to induce us to enter a building and those which persuade us to give it a miss.

'Images yield immense social power . . . (as) potent transmitters of values and ideas.'

George Pattison, *Art, Modernity and Faith*

When it comes to the environment of worship, we should never underestimate the influence of our building upon the way we think about God, about each other, and about the relative importance of the activity we have come together to engage in. Our places of assembly need to speak clearly to us of what we are about as the people of God. Such clarity is required, not only in sign and symbol, but also in the very form and shape of the interior spaces, the texture of the walls and floors, the beauty and excellence of the artifacts we use, look at and handle. God forbid that we should impoverish our environment at the very point and in the very moment when we are in greatest need of every assistance at our disposal to attune ourselves to the presence of God.

'The new reformation (of the liturgical movement) sees architecture as an integral part of the life of the Church, and it has brought about a clearer understanding of the relation between art and religion.'

Nigel Melhuish, *Towards a Church Architecture*, p. 64

'The whole building with its artworks, both inside and without becomes an harmonised canticle or praise, a composite language of prayer.'

Michael Jones Frank, 'Liturgical Art and the Artist', *Church Building* Issue 31

All Christians (even those whose dogmatic formulations tell them otherwise!) are fully aware in daily life of the power of sacramental signs. Exactly why the bunch of flowers should nearly always do the trick, why we can almost hear them speak the words 'I am sorry' or 'I love you', is a total mystery, but it works. Our places of assembly must never become no-go areas for the working out of this universal truth. Art, design, layout, movement, clothing and gesture will all be redolent of powerful meaning quite beyond the delineation of their external attributes. We must recognise this quality in the layout and design of our sacred spaces, and use it to the full.

2. What our buildings say ABOUT us:

The effort (or lack of it) which we ourselves put into the improvement or titivation of our bedsit, our semi, or our office, will tell the world a great deal about us.

What we make of our environment, how we treat it, alter it or decorate it, will speak volumes about what makes us tick and about our priorities in life. In the scruffiest of rooms, a poster stuck on the wall with blu-tack will be a powerful means of non-verbal communication, announcing to any passing coffee-drinker whether we're into animal welfare, equal opportunities, or heavy metal. Indeed, the more modest the pad, the more significant each element becomes, the more effective its message.

Such norms of common daily experience, involving instincts familiar to us all, are for some inexplicable reason left outside at the doorstep by many Christians when entering the building where they gather to worship God. That which is taken for granted in every other walk of life is totally ignored when it comes to giving expression to our religious experience. Caught up in the desire to preserve intact the interior of a church building as a received inheritance, sacrosanct and untouchable, we forget what message these moth-balled interiors communicate to those from outside our community who are sufficiently brave and persistent to enquire within.

All this is of utmost importance for Christians in a post-Christian age, where in our Western materialist society, most people decide (about 85% in England at the last count) not to bother to enquire within. The number of people who stay outside our buildings vastly outnumber those who venture inside. Unless as a Christian Church we want to curl up and die, we need to re-present our buildings in such a way that people first of all are given cause to notice them and secondly are prompted to pop their head inside.

'Bosch looked around the rest of the room. In his job, he learned a lot about people from their rooms, they way they lived.'

Michael Connelly, *The Black Ice* (A Harry Bosch Mystery)

'A young friend went to church close to my home a few weeks ago – the first time since her baptism over twenty years ago. She told me that she will not go again and handed me a list which read: "You are asking me to change the way I speak, the sort of music I enjoy, the length of time I usually listen to a speaker, the type of people I mix with, my body temperature, the type of chair I sit on, the type of clothes I am used to seeing people wear, my sense of humour. You expect me to know when to stand, sit and kneel and the answer to prayers I have never heard. I am prepared to change but there was nowhere I could connect any part of my life with that service."'

Anne Lehanne
Rochester Diocesan newspaper

'People don't go to church because it doesn't even occur to them that they might. It plays no part at all in their weekly life or thoughts.'

Ysenda Maxtone Graham, *The Church Hesitant*, p. 125

'The chief function of any church building is to speak about God, both outside and inside.'

Patrick Brock, *A Theology of Church Design*

'Please do not linger here' Notice in a Wiltshire parish church

'No church building is ecclesiologically innocent: it expresses – and forever thereafter impresses – a sense of what it means to belong to the church, the respective roles of different ministries, the wealth or poverty of the Christian imagination, the sense of where Christ is to be found and so on. It is more than a sermon in stone: it is a multimedia communication of a version of the Christian Gospel, communicated in the shape of the building, its interior arrangements, its decoration and appointments, the kind of interaction it fosters or prohibits among the worshippers. Everything speaks, everything tells us who we are (for better or worse) and what our place is.'

Mark Searle, quoted in *Where we worship* (Huffman and Stauffer), p. 6

Church buildings have ceased by and large to speak clearly of a present reality, and instead convey a mumbled message of a glorious, though faded past. 'For the majority of people in this country, our churches are irrelevant, peripheral and seemingly only concerned with their own trivial pursuits' (Robin Greenwood, *Reclaiming the Church*, p. 156).

A building with grass growing from the gutters and with walls still damp from the last time it rained; last month's porch notices flapping in the wind fixed by a single rusty drawing pin to a rotting notice board; a stack of battered books, spines missing, announcing that God is prayed to in language of the 17th century and sung to in language of the 19th; every inch of floor space taken up with an over-abundant supply of pews, and row upon row of choir stalls defended every Sunday by two blue-robed ladies with processional handbags; a liturgical focus stuck to a wall behind a fence in another room at the far eastern end of the building; brass plaques on everything that doesn't move; no room to swing a cat let alone a censer; all these things SPEAK.

We should not underestimate their message announcing to the passer-by that this kind of building belongs to a group of people who have lost their way, who have forgotten why they meet in this place, who they come to encounter, and what they expect to happen.

When this stage has been reached, the building is no longer a house for the people of God, but merely a valuable but little-used heirloom in the corner-cupboard of our lives.

Reflection: What message does our own church building give to us and to our guests? What impression does it give of the personality and the priorities of our local faith community?

St Procopius' Abbey, Lisle, Illinois.   *Photo: Philip A. Turner*

The building speaks

9

(A) RECALLING THE CHURCH TO THE GOSPEL

Fortunately for humankind, environment is not the only, nor even the primary formative influence in our lives.

'For by one Spirit we were all baptised into one Body – Jews or Greeks, slaves or free – and all were made to drink of one Spirit.'

1 Corinthians 12.13

The Good News that Jesus brings is that everyone has a chance, irrespective of environment. Although shaped by environment, we are not trapped within it.

'Truly I perceive that God shows no partiality, but in every nation any one who fears him and does what is right is acceptable to him.'

Acts 10.34

That which God has set within us, that strange, wonderful unknowable thing we call the grace of God, is the primary influence. Fortunately for us, God is no respecter of persons or of social standing. With him it is impossible to be the wrong colour or hold the wrong passport, and he will come to us where we are, no matter where we are trapped, be it prison cell or commuter train.

'The time is fulfilled and the kingdom of God is at hand; repent, and believe the gospel.'

Mark 1.15

At the heart of the gospel is the message of transformation; the call to be caught up into the life of God, no matter how apparently helpless or hopeless our starting point. Jesus' first recorded words in the earliest Christian gospel summarise the eternal call to change.

'Against all rigid "essentialism" I would immediately add that this essence (of Christianity) shows itself only in what changes.'

Hans Küng, *Christianity: The Religious Situation of our Time*, p. 8

'. . . the continuous apprehension on and on, ever fresh and ever new, of the one inexhaustible God.'

Von Hugel, 'Church and Bible', *Dublin Review* 115

'Growth in the knowledge of God, as all the saints have known, is growth into the unknown.'

David Jenkins, *God, Miracle and the Church of England*

'And Jesus looking upon him loved him, and said to him, "You lack one thing; go, sell what you have, and give to the poor, and you will have treasure in heaven; and come, follow me." At that saying his countenance fell, and he went away sorrowful; for he had great possessions.'

Mark 10.21–22.

This is what deciding to follow Jesus is all about; submitting oneself to a way of life in which nothing is sure or certain or stable or unchanging except the love of God, which remains steadfast through Gethsemane and the Cross. Those who seek certainties and security in this world must look elsewhere, for the essence of Christianity is that paradox between unchanging truth and our continually changing perception of, and experience of, that truth as we gradually 'attain to the unity of the faith and of the knowledge of the Son of God.' (Eph 4.13). Thus, within the security of the love of God we embrace the uncertainties inherent in belonging to a body called constantly to change and to evolve.

A church which panders to humankind's craving for temporal certainties betrays a sickness of the soul, and for this reason the re-ordering of the church building can be the catalyst by which a parish community is recalled to the pilgrim path, to the adventure of going with Jesus into the unknown, to essential Christianity.

If 'moving a few pews around' seems to have a rather tenuous connection with the call of Jesus to discipleship, we need only to recall how astute he was in discerning the grip that possessions and material things had upon those who considered following him. Throughout his ministry, Jesus showed a thoroughgoing sacramental understanding of creation, of the power of the created order either to delight or cripple us. Our goods and chattels are fine, so long as we possess them and not they us.

Church communities are usually quite happy to discuss until the cows come home all aspects of the theory of Christianity, but get nervous when the knife gets near the bone. The point at which the knife goes deepest seems always to concern our possessions; whether our savings or our sanctuaries. It is in these areas the things we have taken to ourselves are seen as being under threat, and the alarm bells ring.

If we want to get to the nub of why re-ordering a church building is a gospel issue, not an architectural one, we might well begin by paraphrasing Jesus' saying in Matthew 6.21 as 'for where your altar rails are, there will your heart be also'. If we can move them we might indeed begin to move heaven and earth.

'A state without the means of some change is without the means of its conservation.'

Edmund Burke

While recognising that environment alone will not transform us, we can at the same time recognise the remarkable and powerful part which our buildings can play in sharpening up for us the basic decision at the heart of the gospel, i.e. 'do we change or do we die?'

David Philippart likens the church building to the 'cookie cutter' which gives particular shape to the lump of pastry on the kitchen table. The church building likewise gives shape and definition to the lump of humanity gathered within its walls, moulding it into the Body of Christ.

'Sacramental space is space which "re-members" the life of the Christian community'

Linley, *Holy People, Holy Space*

Because the re-ordering of a church building, treasured for its familiarity and its memories, requires of us a great deal of letting go, a costly act of surrender, it can be for us a powerful sacrament of God's re-ordering of our whole lives. Re-ordering our building recalls us to the gospel imperative of costly and risk-taking discipleship.

(B) TELLING THE CHRISTIAN STORY TO THE WORLD

We have a story to tell, a short time to tell it in, and limited resources with which to articulate it. Say 'evangelise' to any average group of Christians and they will run for cover, not answering the phone for a whole week in case they have been marked down for that training course on witnessing to Jesus in the street.

'The only hermeneutic of the gospel is a congregation of men and women who believe it and live by it'

Lesslie Newbigin, *The Gospel in a Pluralist Society*, p. 227

'The challenges and opportunities of the Christian churches . . . are to take part in . . . shaping and being shaped by the stories which arise out of the biblical stories in relation to the living of the church in the goings-on of the world.'

David Jenkins, *God, Miracle and the Church of England*

'The eternal word which reorders all creation speaks only local dialects.'

Stephen Cottrell, Liturgy North 96

But wait. Reinforcements are on the horizon. In practically every populated settlement in Britain, a church building stands ready to tell its story. At least the potential is there for story telling, for these buildings are nothing less than the houses of the Church, of the community which by its obedience to Jesus will make his living presence a dynamic reality.

The house of the church can tell a number of different kinds of story. It may restrict itself to archaeology, to history, to architecture, or to an account of its links with a famous son or daughter of that community. We may be shown excellent coloured charts indicating the different periods of construction; or a glass case displaying the great admiral's baptism robe, or a north aisle containing the pram in which the great novelist was first brought to church.

Or a church building can tell the story of creation, of the self-inflicted pain of disobedience; of slavery, exile, and estrangement; of wandering and helplessness; of waiting and longing; of rescue in the person of Jesus, showing us for the first time what it means to be fully human. It can go on to tell the story of the people who down the decades or the centuries have met regularly within its walls to seek the living Lord and to grow in faith and love. It can leave the visitor with something to chew on, something to make them think that perhaps there is something in this Christianity lark after all, if this particular group of people can tell their story with such pride and vigour and delight.

Not for one moment of course does the availability of the church building excuse us from sharing our own individual story of God's love at work in our lives. The building does not let us off the hook but gives us a hook on which to hang our own story. We are not starting from cold any more, or in football parlance, we are no longer kicking-off from the centre spot, but from a free-kick position just outside the penalty box. We have every chance of scoring a goal.

'The Good News, as it relates to our culture, is that being fully human has been demonstrated for us in the person of Jesus Christ, made accessible to us through baptismal incorporation into his death, resurrection, ascension and the gift of the Holy Spirit, and is now being incarnately demonstrated at your local church (or should be).'

Robert Warren, *Building Missionary Congregations*, p. 22

Robert Warren, in his book *Building Missionary Congregations*, shows us that, if we mean to recapture the prophetic dynamic of the gospel in our contemporary culture, we need to show that it is essentially about being human. The layout and design of the congregation's meeting place therefore needs to demonstrate as clearly and as simply as possible the salient features of this dynamic;

– that we are beings-in-relationship rather than creatures in ourselves (and therefore our re-ordered buildings should demonstrate the corporate nature of our worship, repudiating the private cubicle approach summed up by the phrase 'making my communion')

– that we are called to participate (and therefore re-ordered buildings should demonstrate with clarity the exciting re-discovery that the congregation is no longer an audience but is together exercising a shared participatory priesthood)

– that we are a eucharistic, creative and celebratory community living by grace (and therefore our re-ordered buildings should demonstrate in every detail our celebration of life and creation in all its fullness)

The story which the Christian community has to tell does not concern past glories of a bygone age and of doubtful historicity – this is no legend of the Knights of King Arthur's court – but is a tale in which sacred events of the past spill over into the real adventure of the present moment.

The National Trust property at Styal in Cheshire is the most popular in England because this magnificent 18th-century cotton mill continues to burst with life. This is no static display behind a glass case, but is living experience, in which the looms fill the valley with noise, and where, in the apprentices' house, the younger visitors can don 18th century dress and (for a moment at least) get to grips with what it felt like to be a child of 12 rising at 5 am for a long day in the mill.

Apprentice House, Quarry Bank Mill, Styal, Cheshire

'If the material church represents us, it must speak in our language. Unfortunately . . . our weak, nostalgic church architecture reflects well enough the ineffectual, fossilized state of our Christian faith.'

Charles Davis, 'Church Architecture & Liturgy', *Towards a Church Architecture*, p. 115

The story which the church building tells is yet more dramatic than that at Styal Mill, for with us production has never ceased, and as well as looking back we look ahead to all that God will do in us and through us. There is no glass case big enough for God.

Instead, the presentation of our story must be so animated so alive, that our hearers respond by making our story their own, and in due course contribute themselves the next few pages of the never-ending story of God-with-us.

Here then is another reason why re-ordering is an imperative of Christian community life. The external forms we articulate, the layout we choose, the artwork we commission, the relative importance we attach to different parts of the building, the internal arrangements of spaces through which we make the journey of faith each time we gather to worship, all these elements will help us 'make a defence to any one who calls (us) for the hope that is in (us)' (1 Peter 3.15).

This process is not confined to the liturgical areas only, for there is no detail too small to be of significance in what our building says about us. Even the positioning (and the cleanliness!) of the toilets will say something about our community's seriousness about good hospitality and the avoidance of embarrassment for those who come among us.

A miner's lamp hanging before the aumbry. Holy Cross Airedale, West Yorkshire

Parish Rooms toilet, West Yorkshire

'The plan of the church . . . should meet the needs for the celebration of sacred services and also the usual needs in places where people gather together.'

General Instruction of the Roman Missal, 1969, XII, 280

The re-ordered building will thereby help us in every way to tell our story. We need no longer be frightened of evangelism, for we shall find we have been busy doing it, using the building as a sharp and effective tool for our task.

Reflection: Do we as a parish community embrace change as integral to the gospel, or are we fearful of it? In what ways is the process of change readily observed in our use of our building?

PART TWO:
Who are we?

Introduction

'To determine who they truly were, they realised that they must identify with themselves, and in turn project this identification to the outside world.'

Charles King, *Monasticism in the Twentieth Century*, p. 18

'The first step in trying to revitalise the church was to present a vision of what I felt God was calling us to be. Out of this we would discover what he wanted us to do.'

Stephen Cottrell, *Sacrament, Wholeness & Evangelism*, p. 3

We have taken a look in Part One at where we, as God's holy people, have come from, and now need to consider who we are, in order to determine where we go from here. To help us do this, we need to examine our identity as Christians, firstly in the context of contemporary Western culture, and secondly as part of the ever-developing life of the Church. We shall then consider the need for a stategic response which takes note of the various elements of the re-ordering process. Finally we shall consider how to translate ideals into action.

Our culture

10

'We are in the midst of one of those profound upheavals of society when the fundamentals are being shaken, and a new order emerges.'

Robert Warren, *Building Missionary Congregations*

'We no longer say "Cogito ergo sum" (I think therefore I am) but "Tesco ergo sum" (I shop, therefore I am)'.

Photo: *Planning Week*

'Come now, you who say, "Today we will go to such and such a town and spend a year there, doing business and making money." Yet you do not even know what tomorrow will bring.'

James 4.13–14

Contemporary Christian prophets such as Robert Warren have pointed out to us the inescapable fact (attested to by commentators of other faiths and none) that we live in a culture that is disintegrating. Society as we know it is in its death throes, and we live at a time of impending upheaval comparable to the fall of the Roman Empire, the Reformation or the Renaissance.

Humankind is tired of organised religion (though certainly not of spirituality), disenchanted with science, and distrustful of institutions; we have entered a post-Christian era. Nothing can be taken as read; every truth must be dug from the ground all over again, graded, and smelted and hammered out anew.

For the purposes of this book, one particular distinguishing mark may be taken as symptomatic of our contemporary culture; humanity's rediscovery of itself as first and foremost a consumer. While the Christian community has in recent decades been slowly rediscovering its roots and its identity, Western society has not been idle; it has discovered shopping.

On the edge of every major conurbation in Britain, great domed and turreted temples have arisen to which the population may make pilgrimage to worship the great idol of consumer choice. Like the early Christians emerging into the daylight after Constantine, the modern shopper, freed from the constraints of shopping hours regulations, can now enjoy getting and spending all day every day.

Meadowhall, Sheffield
photo: Meadowhall Centre Limited.

'A survey published by market analyst Mintel, predicts that, while relaxing planning controls made the rapid expansion of out-of-town shopping possible in the 1980s, tightening them now has come far too late to save the multitude of small businesses (which have) suffered terminally at the hands of the multiples.'

Planning News, Vol. 3, No. 44, 2 November 1995

The frantic desire to go shopping at all hours of the day and night, in out-of-town shopping malls which, cocooned from the real world, render Leeds indistinguisable from Croydon, appears to be quite uncontrollable. Distance is no object, motorway queuing no discouragement, and doomed city centres trouble us hardly at all. Nothing must be allowed to get in the way of this supreme human activity.

Higher levels of unemployment and an aging population have increased the tendency for shopping to become a leisure activity. Finding a parking place is now impossible *everywhere*.

Although we are in no position as yet to judge the long-term social or moral effects of this major shift in shopping habits, or to assess just how long it will last, what we do know is that it is, at least for the moment, an unassailable fact of life. Unless we regard inculturation as a dirty word, this is the context in which the Christian community must live, and the market pressure to which it must respond.

Within this overwhelming social trend from which none of us is exempt, the triumph of the far-distant supermarket over the corner shop next door, is a particular feature of great significance to the Christian Church in seeking to renew its organisational pattern.

'The shop . . . has large windows and see-through doors, partly so the potential customer can glimpse the goods inside, but equally importantly so that she or he can see the territory into which they are being invited to venture and can weigh-up the emotional risks – how safe the experience is likely to be.'

Peter Cavanagh, *Church Buildings*, p. 5

Over the last few decades, supermarkets have come to dominate food shopping, managing to convert people from the habits of a lifetime and to persuade them to travel considerable distances and to sacrifice both proximity and personal attention for the sake of lower prices, greater choice and anonymity.

In achieving this remarkable revolution, several operational features common to all the major supermarket chains should be noted;

1. Mission; a supermarket chain operates within a clearly defined set of aims (profitability within a

certain sector of the retail market), and nothing will be allowed to divert it from its purpose. All its activities are subservient to this overriding mission.

2. Target group; the supermarket chain analyses with great care and precision the sector of the population it is aiming to attract, and the nature of the goods and services which are likely to appeal to the target group.

3. Specialism; the supermarket chain is not afraid to embrace a particular specialism or 'angle' within the supermarket fraternity, in order to give itself a clear image, thereby helping to distinguish it from its competitors and to help it secure itself a particular niche in the market.

4. Strategy; new stores will be opened on the basis of a clear and well-researched assessment of the size of catchment area necessary to sustain a profitable store, and of a clear policy on the number of stores it wishes to establish in any one region.

5. Location; the supermarket chain will open a store wherever market surveys have established need. By the same token, it will close a store if turnover falls below target level, and will not allow itself to become sentimentally attached to a particular site or to a particular building on that site.

6. Re-building; as needs change or demand grows, a supermarket chain will not hesitate to rebuild its store. Even within a year or two of opening a new store, the chain may rethink its policy (e.g. on restaurant provision) and undertake an extensive rebuilding of the premises.

7. Re-ordering; a supermarket is subject to a constant programme of re-ordering. Sections are rearranged, aisles redesigned and technology updated.

8. Clarity of design; the interior of a supermarket will be an essay in clarity of purpose expressed in good

design, and based on extensive research. The shopper will be led as if by an unseen hand from an attractive entrance area, through a series of spaces and an (apparently sacred) hierarchy of foodstuffs beginning with fruit and vegetables and culminating in wines and spirits. There will be no duplication, and signing and lighting will be excellent.

9. Sell-by date; supermarkets adhere rigidly to sell-by dates in order to ensure that nothing sold on the premises is out of date or in less than prime condition. Lines which have ceased to appeal to customers are promptly withdrawn.

While not all these points will be appropriate to a Christian organisation based on service rather than profit, many of them will be highly relevant to the Church's consideration, within the framework of its strategic planning, of its buildings and how it uses them.

It should be noted that the 'corner shop' approach of established churches such as the Church of England, is diametrically opposed to that not only of major retailers but also of other Christian traditions, such as the Roman Catholic and Pentecostal Churches, which have adopted the 'supermarket' approach of fewer and bigger centres. Centralisation of this kind is also more likely to engender a readiness to view buildings as disposable items in an overall mission strategy.

Before the Church gets too self-righteous about being in a different kind of business, with important considerations other than annual turnover, we would do well to ponder whether our zeal for souls matches the retailers' zeal for success and for good service. Our attitude to our buildings and what we display in them will be a good test of meaning business about our mission.

Reflection: what lessons are there to be learned by the Christian community when considering how major retailers have located and designed their buildings so as to successfully bring about a revolution in shopping patterns?

Exercise: visit as a group a local supermarket belonging to a major chain (preferably one with a cafe!). Go round in pairs observing how the building is made to work by that particular retailer within an overall 'mission strategy'. Meet in the cafe afterwards to discuss how what has been observed differs from the Church's use of buildings as part of its own mission strategy.

Our church

11

'The elements (of Jesus' ritual) are the most commonplace of things, bread and wine, and its original site an upper room in an ordinary structure. Jesus' ritual unites the secular and the holy, implies a continuity between religion and life, proclaims a ubiquitous God, and asserts the possibility that all men may live all their lives in God.'

E. A. Sovik, *Architecture for Worship*, p. 12

'This central event of our faith, in its always renewed eucharistic expression, and at the same time in its intimate contact with the whole of ordinary life, is and remains the specific note which distinguishes the Christian church from any other religious or secular building. All the other qualities or characteristics it has acquired during the almost 2,000 years of its history are not essential to it.'

Frederic Debuyst, *Modern Architecture & Christian Celebration*, p. 20

In the face of the profound upheavals in society around us, what changes are discernible in the life of the Christian community? How is the Church coping with the conflicting demands of being both a counter-culture, offering a new way of life to some extent over against the world, and at the same time a community of love incarnate in the world?

As disciples of Jesus, our privilege in worship is to enter into his prophetic act at his last meal with his first followers, when he used bread and wine to foretell his death and explain his sacrifice. By the constant re-newal of that prophetic act, the Christian community is taken to the heart of the mystery of the death and resurrection of Jesus, the Anointed One of God.

Ever since becoming free to do so in the fourth cen-tury, the Church has considered it essential to provide special places where the assembly could gather and where they could offer together the thanksgiving or eucharist with dignity and with joy.

St Benedict the African, Chicago

'The study of Comparative Religion has fully awakened (us) to the value of the study of 'ritual patterns' for the appreciation of any given system of religious ideas and its necessary consequence in human living – a 'culture'. The analysis of such a pattern and the tracing of its evolution opens for the historian and the sociologist the most direct way to the sympathetic understanding 'from within' of the mind of those who practise that religion'.

Gregory Dix, The Shape of the Liturgy, p. ix

In each era of the Church's development, the ritual patterns developed by each generation and the shape and form of the buildings which housed those rituals, will tell us a great deal about what went on 'under the skin' of those communities.

Throughout Christian history, every fresh insight into the nature and love of God, every reform or revival, has been worked out in bricks and mortar as well as in tracts and texts. What kind of building we meet in, and how it is arranged and decorated for worship, will tell anyone who is interested everything they need to know about us.

Because the buildings we have inherited represent thought-forms of a bygone age, they often present the Christian community with severe problems of identity and communication. Even buildings from the second half of the twentieth century can be a hindrance or an embarrassment.

'The more the real situation evolved in the direction of secularity, the more the church building became aggressively monumental. And it is this very striving for appearance that the twentieth century church has inherited from the nineteenth, and that we still find in the sweeping roofs, dramatic lightings, and enormous stained-glass windows of our pseudo-modern churches.'

Frederic Debuyst, Modern Architecture and Christian Celebration, p. 27

To assess how the Church is responding to these challenges and opportunities, we need to take a look at what is happening in our own generation to our ritual patterns and to the buildings which house them.

In our own generation the Church's most significant response to what both God and the world are saying to us can be seen in what has become known as the Liturgical Movement. This movement has led to an extraordinary renewal in the life, worship and witness of the Church on a scale not seen since the Reformation. The Movement first began to sprout in Belgium in the 1900s, took root firmly in Germany between the Wars, in France during World War II, with new growth eventually being glimpsed in England only after the War.

The Liturgical Movement embraces both worship and the environment of worship; ritual patterns and the buildings which house them. It seeks to address God in language and forms appropriate to our time, in places of assembly which do justice to the theological insights of our day.

Although a few prophetic voices – chief among them Peter Hammond – called us in the 1960s to seize hold of this vision, we in England have been slow learners, resistant to this single currency of a theological liturgical design.*

'The liturgical movement is not a passing fashion but a movement of such force that it amounts to a modern reformation of the Church'

Charles Davis, 'Church Architecture and Liturgy' *Towards a Church Architecture*, p. 111

'The new reformation sees architecture as an integral part of the life of the Church, and it has brought about a clearer understanding of the relation between art and religion.'

Nigel Melhuish, 'Modern Architectural Theory and the Liturgy', *Towards a Church Architecture*, p. 64

Our apparent deafness is symbolised above all in the completion of no less than three gothic cathedrals – Coventry, Guildford and Liverpool – since the Second World War. Time and again we have missed the liturgical boat by failing to think theologically or to start again from first principles. The recent re-ordering of existing cathedrals at Portsmouth and Plymouth are, however, a different story. Here we see a thoroughgoing pursuit of liturgical truth wherever it leads, and the results are breathtaking.

'The Church lives neither by tradition alone, nor by the scriptures directly. The Church lives day by day by her liturgy, which is her living tradition but of which the scriptures are both constituent and normative.'

Eric Mascall (quoted by Patrick McLaughlin), Liturgy & Society, *Towards a Church Architecture*, p. 198

Slowly but surely congregations in this country are catching on, as we begin to appreciate the importance of Liturgical Renewal as a means of bringing about a general revival in the Church's life centred on liturgical action; in other words, the rediscovery of the fact that the Christian community is a liturgical people not a collection of private individuals who occasionally do things together in church.

Our great Public Schools appear to want to perpetuate these quaint archaisms. Pupils of Westminster School, for example, are still required to process daily into the Abbey to be inoculated against Christianity by small regular doses of the Authorised Version and John Bunyan, administered in choir formation.

This is nothing less than liturgical child abuse, and there is urgent need for some bright spark in the Sixth Form to get up a petition to the European Court of Human Rights.

Although architects inspired by the Liturgical Movement recalled us by their new liturgical spaces to the vision of the renewed Christian assembly, they were hamstrung by the liturgy itself. Worshippers in even the most avant-garde building would be required to address God and one another in obsolete language which mocked the best efforts of those attempting to reform the action and redesign the setting of the eucharist.

Post-Reformation polarisation made everyone nervous of letting go of the prayer book or missal which was clutched so tightly as a badge of honour and means of identity. Until a mere 30 years ago (astonishing as it may now seem) we held in our hands each Sunday, orders of service dating from 1570 (for Roman Catholics) or 1662 (for Anglicans). The universal retention of these quaint archaisms of a bygone age had come to acquire doctrinal significance, and adherence to them a litmus test of orthodoxy and ecclesiastical loyalty.

Although the modern Liturgical Movement can be traced back to 1903 and to the newly elected Pope Pius X, it was not until John XXIII called the Second Vatican Council that the pent up flood waters of change engulfed not only the Roman Church but all Christian traditions engaging in liturgical worship.

The Constitution on the Sacred Liturgy (1963) of Vatican II is a watershed of liturgical renewal, and we are all in Rome's debt for recognising that 'it is the liturgy through which, especially in the divine sacrifice of the Eucharist, "the work of our redemption is accomplished", and it is through the liturgy, especially, that the faithful are enabled to express in their lives and manifest to others the mystery of Christ.' (Introduction 2).

The diverse and less centralised nature of the Anglican Communion means that, rather than ripping off the stickingplaster of outdated usage, it has removed it slowly, inch by inch – a much more masochistic way of doing things. Whereas Rome has tackled all aspects of liturgy including the design of liturgical space, the Anglican Communion has restricted itself to the renewal of liturgical texts without mention of the setting in which they are to be used.

In England, the Liturgical Commission of the General Synod has since 1986 produced a series of liturgical resource books to enrich the services of *The Alternative Service Book 1980*, and to help local congregations to rediscover liturgy as a joyous adventure demanding the active participation of every member of the baptised community. In 2000 a new series of volumes under the title *Common Worship* will replace the provisional *ASB*, though sadly not the Book of Common Prayer, our General Synod not having the stomach for the ruthless renewal exhibited by Cranmer himself.

There is a long way to go before our bishops pluck up courage to start talking design (finally letting the cat out of the bag that fenced altars and embroidered hassocks are not after all essential to salvation), but a start has been made.

*Examples of such material are:
Environment and Art in Catholic Worship, produced by the National Conference of Bishops in the United States, Liturgy Training Publications, Chicago 1986;
The Place of Worship, produced by the Irish Episcopal Conference, Veritas Dublin 1966 (revised 1991).

'among the symbols with which liturgy deals, none is more important than the assembly of believers.'

Environment and Art in Catholic Worship, p. 8

'A fully balanced liturgy should enable us to transform our perception of ourselves so that we begin to understand what it means to be sons and daughters of God, images of Christ.'

Michael Jones-Frank, Iconography & Liturgy, p. 32

'Since the entire assembly shares in the priesthood of Christ, the entire assembly celebrates the liturgy'

The Place of Worship p. 8

In the wake of Vatican II the Roman Communion was bolder in approach, totally renewing both liturgy and the layout of the liturgical space. In many countries, the bishops have produced guidelines to help parishes think through theologically the questions surrounding the use and improvement of buildings for worship, seeking to find answers which reflect local culture.* Indeed the *Constitution on the Sacred Liturgy* specifically encourages the provision of 'legitimate variations and adaptations to different groups, regions and peoples, especially in mission countries.' (Ch. I.III D).

Underlying this wealth of new liturgical material whatever its source, is the revelatory insight that it is the people of God themselves, assembled for prayer, who together form the primary icon of Christ among us. We no longer gather merely to gaze at Christ the image of God; in the renewed liturgical assembly we enter into the mystery of *becoming* Christ.

All the faithful should be led to that full conscious and active participation in liturgical celebrations which is demanded by the very nature of the liturgy, and to which the Christian people, 'a chosen race, a royal priesthood, a holy nation, a redeemed people' (1 Peter 2.9) have a right and obligation by reason of their baptism' (*Constitution on the Sacred Liturgy*, Ch. I.II 14).

In this movement of the Spirit we recapture the New Testament vision of the entire Christian assembly as the holy, priestly community called to offer worship. There are to be no more spectators, for in the eucharistic action all the faithful are ministers and celebrants of God's inexpressible gift.

This rediscovery is of treasure which has long lain buried under centuries of theological controversy and mutual suspicion. Previously, both Catholic and Protestant had been too busy grinding their separate axes to acknowledge the truth. The former became obsessed with the ordained priesthood, and the latter with the priesthood of all believers, neither of which can be gleaned from the New Testament.

All that the New Testament tells us about priesthood can be summarised in two basic insights:

(1) that Jesus himself replaces both the priesthood and the sacrifices of the Old Covenant;

(2) that the community of faith, as *a community* not as individuals, shares in that priesthood by virtue of its common Baptism.

'The surest way of bringing home to the laity that they are the Church – and not the passive recipients of spiritual consolation at the hands of a professional ministry – is to make plain the full implications of the eucharistic liturgy.'

Peter Hammond, *Liturgy and Architecture*, p. 168

The local Christian community today lives in exciting times as it digests this truth for itself, and works out how to express it more clearly in everything it says and does and arranges and designs when it meets together to become, by the power of the Spirit, 'a chosen race, royal priesthood, a holy nation, God's own people'. (1 Peter 2.9)

Here then, in this recovered vision of a what it means to BE CHURCH is the Christian response to the call of God and to the pain of a world in crisis.

Reflection: what are the repercussions of this truth for our own local community of faith, as it examines the ways in which the worship space is arranged and the eucharist offered?

Group Exercise:
(1) Discuss what would be the most accurate and appropriate designation for the ordained leader of worship in your community, avoiding any designation which might tend to disenfranchise or disable the eucharistic community as a whole (as well as 'vicar' which speaks of limp lettuce sandwiches). *Animateur*? Team Leader? Co-ordinator? Conductor? Director? Pastor? President? Presider?

(2) Take a look at the floor levels in the existing building, to see whether disparate levels between different ministries within the assembly can be eliminated or avoided. Experiment with the whole of the assembly seated on the same level for the whole eucharist, or possibly moving together to a higher level to stand around the table for the eucharistic prayer.

(3) Experiment in the eucharist with movements and gestures which will serve to underline the shared priesthood of the assembly:
– the whole community processing to the altar at the beginning of the eucharist to kiss the altar in turn
– the whole community standing around the altar for the eucharistic prayer, hands raised with the president in the *orans* position
– at communion, each member of the community holding their portion of consecrated bread until everyone is ready to receive at the same moment (like concelebrants) and communicating themselves from chalices placed on the altar

(4) Experiment with the ordained team leader seated in a distinctive chair but one which is set in the midst of the assembly alongside his/her brothers and sisters, so that he/she *emerges from the community* in order to lead them.

'The earliest posture of the members of the assembly that we know of is standing with arms upraised (usually called the orans *position)'.*

Leonard and Mitchell, *The Postures of the Assembly During the Eucharistic Prayer*

St John Newsome, Huddersfield

Our house

12

'A large room in a private house was evidently, from the Gospel, the first place of worship.'

O'Connor, *Why Revive the Liturgy?*, p. 26

Church of the Nativity, Rancho Santa Fe, San Diego, California

'I should say: the house shelters day-dreaming, the house protects the dreamer, the house allows one to dream in peace.'

Bachelard, quoted by Pollan, *A Place of My Own*

The house of the church which provides a home for the local Christian community will bear the marks of the quiet revolution in thought and practice now enveloping the world-wide Church. Because the Church consists of human beings – themselves a product of a particular culture – its house will also reflect what is going on in society around us. In the United Kingdom at least, the building itself will usually bear the scars (in graffiti or in barred windows) of the disintegration of that culture.

A striking feature of many new buildings of the Roman Catholic Church in the United States is that in their 'commons' or gathering places for the community, they include a great fireplace as a symbol that this is the home of the community.

This echoes the insight of the Focolare Movement (focolare is the Italian word for 'hearth') which, founded in 1944, has sought to live the life of Jesus in ordinary little houses across the world, to bring Jesus to be the 'hearth' of our lives around whom we gather.

These insights take us right back to the beginning when the building for the Christian assembly was known as *domus ecclesiae* – the house of the church, the home of the assembly.

'But will God indeed dwell on the earth? Behold, heaven and earth can not contain thee; how much less this house which I have built!'

1 Kings 8.27

'(In the medieval period) it was called the house of God, and even the "temple" of God before being and showing itself to be the house of the assembly, of God's family.'

Frederic Debuyst, *Modern Architecture & Christian Assembly*, p. 26

Over the centuries we have grown careless in our use of language in this area, talking of the building as the 'house of God' forgetting Solomon's prayer at the dedication of the first temple.

Lord of Peace, Amelia, Ohio

'It is common to use the same name to speak of the building in which (the believers) worship, but that use is misleading.'

Environment and Art in Catholic Worship, p. 8

'The church building is the house of the church . . . the house of the people who are themselves the temple of the living God. It has no meaning apart from the community it serves.'

Peter Hammond, *Liturgy and Architecture*, p. 28

As already noted, we have also gone along with the custom of using the same word to describe both the assembly – the church – and for the building in which the assembly meets. We have thereby greatly de-valued the New Testament concept of the assembly of believers as the living stones of the new temple not made with hands, and we urgently need to restore it to its primary place in our vision of God's call to us.

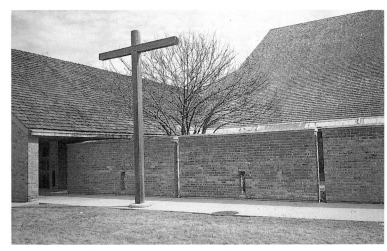

St John of the Cross, Western Springs, Illinois

In this task we shall have to peel away the many accretions which have through the centuries gradually obscured the essential nature of the Christian liturgical assembly, accretions which are basically intrusions from a pre-Christian understanding of the sacred, concerned primarily with objects rather than persons.

As in the case of the role of the co-ordinator of the assembly's worship, what we really need is a new word to describe our building. Perhaps 'house' or 'home' would give us a clue, taking us back to the domestic era of church architecture in the first three centuries. This is a direction in thinking reinforced by the work of architects such as Edward Dart in Chicago, and can be seen in this country in such recent buildings as the Chapel of Reconciliation at Walsingham which, although not domestic in scale, sits comfortably and modestly in its rural setting, a model of architectural inculturation.

Chapel of Reconciliation, Walsingham, Norfolk

Such an approach gives architectural expression to Jesus' teaching that the Christian community is to be leaven working silently but effectively within the dough of society, and it is an approach appropriate to a post-Christian era in which understatement can be more telling than declamation.

'In recent times the Church has made clear her preferential option for the poor, so the design and development of this church reflect this, while not preventing it from being a worthy place for the celebration of the liturgy.'

Austin Winkley, *Church Building Issue 8*, Winter/ Spring 1988

In this country we can see the same movement expressed in the many new houses of the church built to a domestic scale. Typical of this genre is St Theodore's, Hampton-on-Thames (1984) described by its architect as being 'like a tent'. So successful was its expression of domestic scale that several enquiries were received during the construction period from prospective purchasers seeking a new house in the area.

St Benedict, Garforth, Leeds. Vincente Stienlet 1998

If as a community of faith we are taking a fresh look at our home in this process, if we now have an opportunity of considering a major refurbishment, we need to ask the basic question 'What do we want our building to achieve for us? How can it more clearly express our priorities and our communal lifestyle?'

This gets us off to a good start because it reverses the usual set of assumptions in which we end up considering what we can do to better serve the building. We need to remember that it is the building which is the servant, and the assembly the master whose needs always must come first. The whole point of being a people living in tents is that we need never be afraid of God's call to move on. We never lose our heart to a particular camp-site, remaining at the ready to pick up our tent and walk.

As we set about refurbishing our own house of the church, we find that we are engaged in a process in which both theology and evangelism play their part.

(1) THEOLOGY

The process of re-ordering will help us primarily in discovering who we are as a community of faith, and where we came from. Re-ordering helps us refresh our collective memory, through which we shall recover our sense of identity and purpose.

The thing that will make our house of the Church special, and fascinating, and different and fun, will be the story it tells which, if we tell it straight, will be unique. There are two basic parts to this story of ours:

(a) the story we share with all other Christians – the story of creation, disobedience, slavery and rescue, culminating in the person and work of Jesus, the Anointed One, the Exalted Lord, who in the power of the Spirit leads us home to the Father.

(b) the story of this particular group of people, living and departed, who have prayed and worked and laughed and cried in this place on their pilgrimage of faith.

Although the first part of the story will be known to many, we must not assume that it will be known to all who enter our building. As the reality of our de-Christianised and multi-cultural society sinks in, we are rapidly reaching the stage when the Christian story will be known to comparatively few, and will need to be re-told again and again with fresh clarity and vigour. Even among committed Church members, there is widespread ignorance about the basic facts of our Christian story.

Alongside the preaching and instruction of the Church, the catechumenate, and our community's library of books and tapes, the internal arrangement of the building where we meet stands ready to become a teaching aid of prime importance.

(2) EVANGELISM

The context in which we take stock of our own building – that 'local centre for worship and mission' – is one of a critical missionary situation in which time is short.

As a boy I used to love saving my pennies in the little CMS Lent box made in the shape of an African mud hut, doing my bit to help the missionaries. Fifty years on the roles are reversed; England is recognised as one of the stoniest and most heart-breaking bits of evangelistic ground in the world, and Africans are now saving up their pennies to come and preach the gospel to us.

'In that context, a church which does not grow will die'.

Nigel McCulloch, Bishop of Wakefield. Diocesan Synod Address, 19 June 1993

In 1993 the Diocese of Wakefield became the first English diocese to be designated a 'missionary diocese' in England, in recognition of its position nearly at the bottom of the league table for church attendances (18 per 1000 adults) and in the hope of bestirring the diocesan family to face facts and to roll up its sleeves.

'If the layman has learned to accept his responsibilities as a member of an organic, priestly community, and as an active participant in the eucharist, this awareness will undoubtedly be reflected in due course in his whole attitude towards the Church and its apostolic mission in the contemporary world'

Peter Hammond, *Liturgy and Architecture*, p. 168

'The spectacle offered by our existing churches is depressing. A neglect of

Crucial to our ability to respond to the call to growth and development is a willingness to start again with our buildings. This is no time to parade our prejudice

the liturgy and a defective understanding of it resulted in churches but imperfectly adapted to the needs of liturgy and, indeed, has often put many obstacles in the way of its proper celebration.'

Charles Davis, 'Church Architecture and the Liturgy', *Toward a Church Architecture*, p. 110

'A church has to be an authentic image of a living and active community that has a message for the present world.'

Charles Davis, 'Church Architecture and the Liturgy', *Toward a Church Architecture*, p. 115

or personal preference, and we can no longer allow our houses of the Church to proclaim on the outside decay and disinterest, and on the inside, worship as a spectator sport, and an extremely boring one at that. All Christian communities need to put their house in order, some may even have to leave home.

If we mean business in this field, the vast majority of our parish churches will require radical re-ordering to refurbish and re-equip them for service in the next century.

Even those churches which have been reordered recently must likewise be subject to this need for constant reappraisal, for re-ordering is a continual process not a one-off event.

A paradigm of this unceasing process is the Benedictine Abbey Church of La Pierre-Qui-Vire in Burgundy, the 'engine room' of liturgical renewal in France. The Abbey is now onto its fourth re-ordering scheme in 20 years, fine-tuning the building to the community's needs until it runs smoothly and sweetly. Re-ordering is a cyclical process, as experiment stimulates improved use, and regular use reveals the need for further experiment.

In this way is the house of the church finely honed to serve as perfectly as possible the needs of the worshipping community. In this way too the house of the church becomes a home.

Reflection:
(a) What word should we use to best describe the role of our building in the life and work of our community?

The Re-ordering of LA PIERRE-QUI-VIRE

Phase One 1955

Phase Two 1967

Phase Three 1976

Phase Four 1993

(b) In what practical ways could we make our house of the church more like a home?

Exercise: To help clarify who is the boss around here:

(1) Draw up a shopping list of all the activities which the faith community wishes to organise within this building. Please note that this list is not a list of all existing activities, but of those the community would wish to see in operation arising from its Mission Statement in the context of its Strategic Development Plan (see chapter 13). Some activities will be entirely new – uses which the building in its old form has not allowed you to accommodate because of its un-suitability.

Some existing activities will ease because drawing up your SDP has allowed you to re-assess them in the light of your Mission Statement. Uses which give wrong messages (e.g. jumble sales which suggest that the community's finances depend on haphazard events instead of on direct giving), or which prove unproduc-tive (e.g. uniformed organisations which tear the place apart but which take no real place in the worshipping life of the community), may well have to go.

(2) Draw up a list of the accommodation – room sizes, special requirements etc – which each of the agreed activities will require, and match it up on a large sheet of paper with the accommodation which the building at present offers. It is of course important to include worship space in this exercise; just because worship is already accommodated in the building does not mean that it is accommodated satisfactorily or helpfully. Compare the two!

(3) Assess the level of refurbishment or reconstruc-tion required to make the existing building a fitting home for the people of God in this place, a home to which the community is proud and delighted to invite its friends and from which it can work effectively in pursuance of its Mission Statement.

13

Our strategy

Having taken stock of our church building in the context of our culture, of the Church's redefined role in society, and of the particular circumstances of our own patch, how should we respond to the opportunities before us? The world has thrown down the gauntlet; can we rise to the challenge? Can we for once actually come up with a plan, rather than simply a knee-jerk reaction?

The Church is very good at thinking on its feet and responding effectively to crises, but very bad at strategic thinking, seeing the broad canvas, reading the signs, remaining one step ahead. It tends to be a reactive, if not reactionary, body.

In the Church of England, the recent 'coming of age' of the parish church, now required at last to stand on its own feet financially like any other grown-up, is concentrating the mind wonderfully. Unless the parish community learns to think strategically it will go to the wall, or at very best survive only as someone else's occasional outpost.

'We need to recognise the downside of the church in pastoral mode within our new missionary setting and taking with us the good things from that mode, find new ways of being church.'

Robert Warren, *Building Missionary Congregations*, p. 4

To enable the community to switch from maintenance (or pastoral) to mission mode, and to plan for growth as a matter of course, it will need to undertake a thoroughgoing Parish Audit and, on the basis of the audit, to draw up and formally adopt a STRATEGIC DEVELOPMENT PLAN.

The formulation of such a plan will help the local Christian community realise the need for a more robust and risk-taking life-style appropriate to a missionary situation. Freed from the concept of going to church, it will begin to discover new ways of being church.

In the formulation of a Strategic Development Plan (SDP), the following questions will need to be addressed:

1. Theological Base

Everything we do should flow from theology, not from expediency (responding to this week's panic) or tradition (being blackmailed by the church council bully). The community needs to take time to consider its calling under God in a relaxed prayerful atmosphere where it's not watching the clock. Here again a parish week-end is a necessity, not a luxury, and an acid test of whether people mean business.

Each parish community will have its own theological starting points, language, and instincts, with which to draw up a MISSION STATEMENT that will encapsulate its chief concerns and aims in a style completely its own. The community should put out of its mind the details of the mission statement of that parish the bishop seems to think so highly of. Instead it needs to ask the question, 'what do *we* need to say, *here* in this place?'

2. Buildings Strategy

Maintenance of buildings is the biggest single headache of most church councils, so strategic thinking is needed to cure it. The clue is to start with the strategy not with the building. Certain questions need to be asked:

'Since 1990 we have witnessed in the Church of England alone the planting of around 30 new church communities every year, nearly all of which will have begun their life in borrowed buildings.

George Lings, co-author of the General Synod Report *Breaking New Ground* (GS 1099) May 1994

In 1974, the parish of Bradley, Huddersfield, abandoned its Victorian building (on the wrong side of the A62) and relocated in the middle of the housing estates it sought to serve. No prizes for architecture, but a gold medal for missionary endeavour.

Bradley Parish Church:

. . . old

. . . new

(a) Does the community need to *own* a building? The explosion in the number of church planting projects is the latest nudge from the Holy Spirit as to the direction in which healthy communities of faith should follow. If mission is the community's top priority, then there is much to be said for operating out of a 'user-friendly' building already familiar to the people we are trying to reach. A neighbourhood school is a good example. Hiring a local school provides excellent facilities for both worship and nurture in groups, at a fraction of the cost of maintaining a building of our own. It is an object lesson in travelling light.

(b) Does the community need *this* building, i.e. the one it has inherited from previous generations of Christians operating in very different circumstances? Sometimes to close an existing building and to move to another site will be the right and courageous thing to do. Alternatively the building can be kept as a week-day chapel and administrative centre, while the main activity of worship and outreach is transferred elsewhere.

(c) From what location in the parish should the Christian community be seeking to operate if its first priority is the implementation of its Mission Statement? What possibilities are there for hiring existing premises or for new-build in that particular area?

(d) Do the answers to any of the above questions prompt the community to consider using their existing building for a different purpose in their SDP, or for disposing of it altogether through initiating the redundancy procedure?

(e) How many buildings does the community require to best carry out its Mission Statement? If there is at present more than one (e.g. a parish hall as well as a building for worship), should the uses be combined on a single site and the surplus building sold or converted to another use within the context of the SDP?

(f) Are there buildings belonging to other Christian traditions in your parish? If so, what scope is there for combining operations out of a single building strate-gically placed?

(g) If the existing building is to be retained, what alterations will be necessary to re-equip it as a fitting place of assembly for worship and a suitable oper-ational base for the community's other activities?

3. Growth Strategy

Growth and development need to be assumed from the outset, and a careful analysis made of how mem-bers of the existing community came to faith. Likely sources of further growth can then be identified, and plans drawn up over a five year period to concentrate resources in these areas.

For example, mission teams might be formed, each to work with a different sector of the local population – e.g. students, old people, lapsed members, or mothers and toddlers – to assess the needs of each sector and to prayerfully initiate a plan of action to draw them into the community of faith.

4. Business Plan

Although the Church is more than a human organisa-tion, it is not less than one, and has no excuse for operating in anything other than a thoroughly profes-sional and businesslike manner.

Where possible, the Church should pinch the devil's best tricks as well as his best tunes by adopting skills and insights learned the hard way by organisations operating in the fields of public service and commerce. In these times of economic stringency, any proven system for deepening unity of purpose and increasing efficiency warrant close examination.

Business or service planning might cover:
– the aims and objectives of the association (faith community);
– how the association currently fulfils these

- the areas and constraints within which the association aims to meet the needs for the future, and some assessment of these needs
- the range of options open to the association to meet these needs with a preferred strategy
- how this strategy will be implemented, the level of resources required and where these will come from
- targets against which the performance of the association can be measured

Detailed notes on preparing an operational plan can be found in Appendix E.

Talk of 'objectives' and 'targets' will be anathema to many Christians, but we should be more fearful still of a Church with an unaccountable leadership and a direction which is literally aim-less. Spirituality is a means not of evading the need for efficient working, but of giving it new purpose as we straighten the path for the Kingdom of God.

'If you don't have a business plan, how do you know what you want to achieve and how you are going to do it? Too many managers will respond – oh it's all in my head – but unless it's written down, how will you make decisions about where to put your resources; which development opportunities to pursue; whether staff resources are being used most effectively.'

Wendy Murphy, *To plan or not to plan?*, p. 27

5. Finance

Sooner or later the question of finance will be asked of the dreamers of daydreams; how do we pay for all this? In fact experience shows that finance follows vision as night follows day; it is vision, not money, that is in short supply.

Nevertheless, long term financial planning is necessary for any community wishing to move forward, and we need to stop budgeting for survival and start budgeting for growth. If tackled in a manner which is both prayerful and business-like, an appropriate re-ordering can be brought within the grasp of any Christian community. Some notes on fundraising can be found in Appendix F.

These are just a few of the ways in which the local church community can begin to operate more effectively in making its mission statement a reality. Strategic planning is not a magic wand to wave over our problems to make them disappear, but offers us a *modus operandi* which will help give us some credibility in the eyes of those who watch and wait to see what the Church is made of. If we can remove efficiency from the Church's list of dirty words, then we shall have made a start and, at a time when the world dismisses the Church as an irrelevance, have done our own confidence no harm at all.

Reflection: Is my own Christian community proactive, re-active, or just plain reactionary? How in our particular situation can we find new ways of being church?

Exercise: Answer in your group questions (a) to (g) above.

14 Elements of re-ordering (1)

PROCLAIMING GOOD NEWS

In formulating a buildings strategy as an integral part of a Strategic Development Plan, we find that certain elements can be discerned as constants in the re-ordering process. They will help us re-pitch the tent in a good camp-site. The building's capacity for proclamation is the first of these elements.

*'A Communications Audit.'
Communications Unit Church House 1995

'What is your church's message?' is a question asked of all Anglican parishes in a leaflet produced by the Church of England's Communications Unit.*

'If you are going to build a church you are going to create a thing which speaks. It will speak of meanings, and of values, and it will go on speaking. And if it speaks of the wrong values it will go on destroying.'

Robert Maguire, 'Meaning and Understanding', *Towards a Church Architecture*, p. 66

It is a question that every Christian community should ask in relation to its own building, for in a missionary situation we cannot afford buildings which subvert our task of proclaiming Good News. The church's building is a commanding preacher, and no one should underestimate its power to communicate. Its message can linger on long after our own words have died away. Buildings, no less than people, have a body language; to quote Ralph Waldo Emerson, 'What you are speaks so loudly I can't hear what you say'.

'There is still today a kind of general belief that the church has to be an external sign intended to symbolise Christianity in the modern city . . . a notion still considered to be a "constant" of Christian architecture. In fact, it could be valid only

Most church buildings inherited from previous generations will have been conceived as monuments in which external form is of greater significance than internal arrangement (*interiority* made subject to *monumentality* in the words of Debuyst). We shall need to consider the appropriateness of this historical stance in a post-Christian era, and look at ways of re-presenting our buildings in ways which make good sense in our present cultural setting. If we are serious

St Augustine, Darlington (Fenwick Lawson)

within an integrally Christian context, in which society, city, surroundings were one.'

Frederic Debuyst, *Modern Architecture & Christian Celebration*, p. 28

'The visual surroundings and forms are not only formative but also witnessing. They preach.'

Frank Kamarcik, *The Beraka Award 1981*

'Abandon hope, all ye who enter here . . .

'Not today, thank you . . .'

about sharing good news, we need to find ways of converting palaces into homes.

In re-presenting our buildings, there are several elements we need to consider:

(a) Exterior Shape and Form

Before ever a hand is laid upon the door handle, the house of the church will have made an impact from a distance by its outline and basic shape. This impact can either encourage further enquiry or cause the building to be dismissed from further consideration.

If our community has inherited an old building from a previous generation, there is not a lot we can do about its basic form and shape, even though in many cases these basic attributes will give out all the wrong signals. Apart from causing us some embarrassment, such buildings can be a real handicap in persuading others to take us seriously as a living community with something vital to say.

We can however learn from the many examples of new houses of the church which proclaim a message complementary to, rather than contradictory of, the life and work of the local Christian community. Such buildings also help us to rethink our concept of what a sacred building should look like in this post-Christian era, and what symbolism is appropriate to it.

In Edward Dart's design for the monastic church of the Benedictine community of S. Procopius Abbey, Lisle, Illinois (1971), we see a church building whose external shape and form is in itself a teaching aid, a sign so redolent of powerful images from scripture and tradition, that additional 'labelling' (eg with a cross) is rendered supefluous. The east end of the

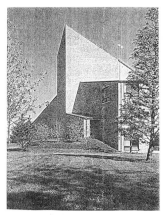

'the prow of the ark of God'
– S. Procopius Abbey, Lisle,
Illinois

'*Seen from a distance, the
St Procopius Abbey
Church is a dramatic
statement in brick and
glass on a wooded Illinois
hillside . . .
A 17-foot cedar cross near
the main entrance is the
exterior symbol of the
monastery's religious
nature.*'

Lane & Kezys *Chicago
Churches and Synagogues*,
p. 214

abbey church rises from surrounding woodland like a prow of a great ship, the Ark of God.

Few of us however get to build a new house for the Church; most of our time is spent breathing new life into old ones, grappling with the shape and form of buildings bequeathed to us irrespective of our views on the matter. In this situation we need to:

(i) reassess the building's appropriateness for us today in the context of a Buildings Strategy (see chapter 13), facing up to whatever hard decisions are called for (even redundancy).

(ii) test out the building's effect on others by inviting members of a parish community from another diocese to visit our parish and assess the impact of our building on someone approaching it for the first time. What are the signals it is sending out?

(iii) use every means available to 'repackage' the building, and present it in the best possible light; by architectural re-styling (e.g. a new entrance area), by landscaping, floodlighting, signing, stone-cleaning or a good old-fashioned spring clean.*

(b) Interior Space

Although it will come as something as a shock to most members of our church communities, the interiors of the vast majority of our houses of the Church are a living liturgical nightmare.

They are cluttered spaces devoid of space and full to overflowing with furniture, displaying a total visual confusion of purpose, enshrining as sacrosanct liturgical divisions and practices which have long ceased to have any theological meaning, temples of prejudiced conservatism and repositories for threadbare furnishings which we would have discarded from our own homes years ago.

* FOOTNOTE: Where new building work on an ecclesiastical building is involved, consult a VAT specialist at an early stage, to maximise the amount of work that can be zero rated.

'The majority of Gothic-revival churches are unsuitable for twentieth-century worship not simply because they are often full of unlovely ecclesiastical furniture and sentimental stained glass, or because they have ill-proportioned altars and dreadful sculptured reredoses. Their unsuitability above all is due to the fact that they are planned in accordance with an understanding of the liturgy which is fundamentally at variance with modern biblical and liturgical scholarship.'

Peter Hammond, *Liturgy and Architecture*, p. 137

We have grown accustomed to these things, and are blinded to their impact on others. To those who come fresh to an experience of worship however, or to those who have caught a vision of just how stimulating and beautiful liturgical space can be when we let go, these tired old interiors can appear at best sad and pathetic, at worst an affront to God.

In most cases the interiors of our buildings are areas where worshipping communities are free, within the framework of the faculty jurisdiction or equivalent structures, to achieve a complete transformation of the house of the church. Such physical transformation can be a catalyst for the transformation of the community itself, a sacrament which makes real that which it signifies.

'The problem is that the building's intrinsic spatial characteristics are often, perhaps most often, obscured by an overlay of strenuous furnishing.'

Robert Maguire, Liturgy North 96

The only pre-requisite is the worshipping community's act of will to tackle this communication problem, but no cure can take place until the patient accepts that help is needed. The treatment will be wide-ranging, as we shall see in the the following pages, but a useful first step would be to invite an informed group of Christians from some distance away to give an honest first impression of how it felt to walk into our building, and what message the building spoke to them.

'Following our visit to the refectory, we wandered through the delightful maze comprising the rest of the Abbey, where at every corner we sensed a new visual surprise . . .'

(St Procopius Abbey)
Charles King *Monasticism in the Twentieth Century*, p. 22

(c) Progression of Spaces

The internal arrangement of spaces will speak not only of movement (or lack of it) but also of the story of a community of faith; how the community understands itself and the ministries entrusted to it.

Clear demarcation and discreet but clear signing will help the newcomer discern the nature of the community and its chief characteristrics. Examples of this might be the way in which a community has celebrated its rediscovery of baptismal vocation by moving its font into a prominent position and creating a baptistry of space and dignity, or has marked its greater awareness of the need for Christian nurture by creating a narthex where people can meet and socialise.

Such demarcation can often be achieved by the relocation of dividing screens, removing them from positions where they obscure the liturgical action or reinforce an out-dated and hierarchical understanding of the liturgy, and resiting them in positions where demarcation is useful. In this way a rood screen might be removed from the chancel arch (where division is no longer appropriate) and placed across the westernmost bay to demarcate a narthex from the nave (where division is actually needed).

(d) Inculturation

Because such an important part of our story is our response to the story of God's love for us, it is vital to make the place of assembly redolent of our history and culture.

This is why symbolism should never be mass-produced and why we need to incorporate within the interior design of the worship space clear references to local characters and events.

St Paul, Willington Quay, Wallsend

A display of photographs in the gathering place of all the parish community, not just the leadership team, is a wonderful introduction for the visitor to this particular 'house of the church'. The thought of 'being personal' makes the English extremely nervous, but we must get a grip on ourselves lest we impoverish the interiors of our buildings and deprive ourselves of colour and interest. We need to get better at 'being personal' and celebrating the local and the particular in the midst of our assemblies.

(e) Recording History

When the community of St Thomas' Huddersfield removed the stone pulpit from its Victorian building in 1990, much fruitless effort was expended on trying to remove the resultant cement marks from the pier of the chancel arch before it was realised that to leave the discoloration would in fact help tell the story.

So the discoloration remains as a kind of 'high tide mark' of Victorian clutter, a reminder of changed priorities in the Church over the last 100 years, and already a useful talking point for visitors when being shown around.

St Clement, Leigh-on-Sea

Our ancient buildings are full of such detail, as the Church at some point changed course and left a particular feature high and dry – like those rood loft doorways now leading nowhere except to a 20ft drop. Leave such anachronisms to help us tell our story, but give a little help from our own generation in the form of well designed and discreet signing and explanation. In this way we shall remember where the tents used to be pitched before we moved camp.

Reflection: How might our community improve or adapt its existing building to complement the work of proclaiming good news?

Exercise: Take a walk round your own house of the Church, both outside and in, and identify ways of improving its storytelling technique in the work of Christian proclamation.

St Francis, Long Eaton. *Photo: Martine Hamilton-Knight*

15

Elements of re-ordering (2)

CHRISTIAN NURTURE

In the Church between the 4th and 7th centuries . . . 'the mode of fixing of the memory and the mechanisms of recall were consolidated into visual and aesthetic data.'

Patrick Reyntiens, *Tablet*, 1 Jun 96

'Of their nature the arts are directed toward expressing in some way the infinite beauty of God in works made by human hands.'

Constitution on the Sacred Liturgy, VII, 122.

'We have forgotten who and what we are, and art makes us remember.'

G. K. Chesterton

'Diocesan Advisory Committees should usually turn down any proposal for more stained glass in a church . . . the absence of stained glass is a great aesthetic advantage. Where the glass is not positively good, it is an irrelevance, if not an embarrassment.'

Alec Clifton-Taylor, *English Parish Churches as Works of Art*, p. 152

A re-ordered house of the church can be a vehicle not only for proclaiming good news, but also for nurturing the faithful by recalling the liturgical assembly to its identity and to its task.

Art is an invaluable tool in this didactic task, and it is encouraging to note the fact that symbolism is no longer an issue – icons are everywhere and candles blaze away in nearly every cathedral in the land. Even pieces of sculpture pop up in surprising ecclesiastical locations. Christians, whatever their background, no longer seem afraid of art.

Art is particularly important in teaching the faith because it can stimulate our sense of devotion simply by reminding us of who we are and of how far we have travelled together; it keeps our collective memory fresh. For this reason art provides an irreplaceable means of giving character and colour to liturgical space.

Symbolism will remain one of the most potent ways in which a community can tell its story, proclaim the beauty of God's creation, and reaffirm its own identity. Great care should be taken to avoid inserting 'bits of art' merely to decorate a blank wall, fill up an empty corner or (worst of all) subject a worshipping community to doom and gloom by inserting yet more stained glass, that most overrated of all Christian art forms.

St Stephen Walbrook 'before'

St Stephen Walbrook 'after'.

St Margaret, Brightside, Sheffield. Martin Purdy 1995

The Hayes Conference Centre, Swanwick, Derbys. Liturgical Space for Chester Clergy Conference 1998. Richard Giles with Christopher Hewetson.

t Edmund, Forest Gate,
ondon E7.
Cottrell & Vermeulen 1994
Photo: Edward Woodman)

St Julie Billiart, Greater Chicago.
Guy Prisco.

Santa Maria Supra Minerva,
Assisi.

Plymouth Cathedral. Anthony Harrison 1994

The work of
William Schickel.

St Anne's Convent,
Melbourne,
Kentucky.

The Chapel, Grailville, Loveland, Ohio.

St Thomas Huddersfield. Richard Giles 1990

Sherbourne Abbey: West Window (detail)
John Hayward 1998

The Venerable Bede, in St Paul, Jarrow.
Fenwick Lawson 1973

Nancy Chinn,
watercolour on nylon.

Photos: Liturgy Training Publications, Chicago.

South Creake, Norfolk

Art in the place of liturgical assembly should complement the liturgy itself, entering into the dialogue between God and his people.

Further notes on the use of art in worship, and the selection of artists, can be found in Appendix B. At this point we simply need to note that if we are setting out to proclaim good news of God, then art will be an indispensible help to us in our task.

Art remains however merely a tool in the hands of the church community, and one which we must learn to handle with care, respecting its capacity to damage as well as to delight. Art, together with all other tools at our disposal, must be subject to liturgical principles if it is to fulfil a didactic role and enable the house of the Church to speak to us with clarity and purpose.

(a) Avoidance of Clutter

A vivid memory of mine is of seeing the great nave of Ely Cathedral completely empty of chairs, revealing a vast space which allowed the architecture to speak with powerful clarity.

The biggest single enemy in the re-ordering of our worship spaces is gothic clutter. It is bad enough that every square inch of the floor area of our buildings must be occupied with furniture, chiefly acres of pews, worse still that the furniture must be covered with foliated tracery, thereby establishing beyond all reasonable doubt that such items are sufficiently 'churchy' to be allowed in an ecclesiastical building.

If nature abhors a vacuum, the English at worship abhor space, with silence coming a close second. Much frantic effort is devoted to filling in as rapidly as possible, space in our liturgical rooms and silence in our liturgies. We are uncomfortable before them. If there is a silence, we immediately assume the leader has lost his or her place in the book; if space, that thieves have been busy the night before.

Chelveston,
Northamptonshire

'One of Suffolk's stateliest
churches, Blythburgh, has
no Victorian nor modern
glass at all, and as a result
is flooded with light and,
sometimes sunshine,
falling with splendid effect
on to the white walls and
pinkish brick floor.'

Alec Clifton-Taylor, *English
Parish Churches as Works of
Art*, p. 152

In fact, the creation of space as an essential element of re-ordering is of great significance and value. The horizontal emphasis of any sizeable floor area uninterrupted by furniture has a restful effect which recalls us to tranquility of spirit in a frantic world. It is an antidote to busy-ness, and at a time when every square metre of floor area has to justify its existence, the sheer extravagance of space can remind us of the extravagant love of God.

Light streaming in through clear leaded windows will likewise recall us to God's generosity, create a space of great openness and beauty, and help avoid the visual clutter and busyness of an interior overpowered by Victorian stained glass.

The visual overcrowding of our liturgical spaces is evident not only in buildings designed for Sunday worship, but overflows into every possible ecclesiastical outpost, where confined spaces magnify the ill effects of our bad habits. Seek out the chapel of any institution – hospital, school, or conference centre – and you will find it full to the brim with Victorian pews, prie-dieu, presidential chairs (various), credence table and other bric-a-brac.

Such overcrowding is all the more critical in view of the simplicity demanded of liturgical spaces like these, in order to achieve the more intimate atmosphere appropriate to the scale of the room. As we shall see in chapter 25, such liturgical spaces require a ruthlessness in inverse proportion to their size.

A very useful exercise for a worshipping community to undertake is to wait for a very sunny Saturday and to move out into the church yard every single piece of furniture that will move or unscrew. The effect is liberating, especially if the nave can be cleared, for the

'The strong and elemental openness of liturgical place makes for dynamism and interest. It is a vigorous area for conducting public business in which petitions are heard, contracts entered into, relationships witnessed, orations declaimed, initiations consummated, vows taken, authority exercised, laws promulgated, images venerated, values affirmed, banquets attended, votes cast, the dead waked, the Word deliberated, and parades cheered.'

Aidan Kavangah *Elements of Rite* quoted by Barbara Barnum, Liturgy North 96

building in all its spaciousness is seen for the first time. It is only then that the community realises just how much space it has at its disposal in which to move about, and to tell its story, and bring to life the mystery of faith, Christ in us. We will have to put it all (or very nearly all!) back again of course, at least for the moment, but it's heaven to be king of our building, if only for a day.

(b) Avoidance of Duplication

There is a house of the church in the Wakefield Diocese which until recently boasted no fewer than four fonts. As through the centuries improvements were made and a new font provided as part of the latest renovation scheme, no one had the heart to throw out the previous one. So the collection grew.

This may be an extreme example, but there are not many buildings for worship in this country that are untainted by the sin of duplication.

We take it for granted, for example, that there will be more than one altar in the house of the church; that if a nave altar is introduced the high altar will remain, and probably at least one other in a side chapel or two.

The moment we stop to think about it, we realise that to have more than one altar in a worship space is of course quite bizarre. Unthinkable in the first few centuries of Christian history, and making no sense at all to us once we consider the theological implications of what we are doing and the confused message that our cluttered interior is giving out.

A community of faith needs one altar, and one only, around which to gather on Sundays and Festivals. In parishes where it is the tradition to celebrate the eucharist on weekdays, it may be necessary to have a second altar in a separate room suitable for small groups to worship in, mainly for practical reasons of heating in winter (but see chapter 25). In no circumstances should more than one altar be visible within a single worship space.

If the retention of the high altar is made a condition – by a pressure group within the parish (or even by a DAC or other outside body) – then the church community should have the courage to decline the offer of a half-baked scheme. Let the nave altar wait until the community of faith has worked through its understanding of its vocation and its purpose at a few more parish weekends, and until such a head of steam has built up that nothing and no one will be allowed to get in the way of progress.

We should never be pushed into muddled half-measures; any re-ordering we underake should display a striking clarity of liturgical purpose arising from sound theological principle.

The same will apply to the place for the reading and preaching of the Word of God. We have grown accustomed to having at least two points – lectern and pulpit – for this single liturgical purpose, and that is one too many. The community needs to take its time to consider where in the area of assembly is the best position for the reading and preaching of the Word, and construct there an ambo for the purpose. This may consist of either lectern or pulpit repositioned and adapted for the purpose, but it is more likely to require a new piece of furniture and the disposal of both our old favourites.

The problem of duplication lurks everywhere – in presidential chairs lined up in the sanctuary, in crosses here, there and everywhere, in litany desks by the dozen. In nearly every case all we need is one, and in the other cases none at all. Ruthlessness is required. Bon courage!

Ss. Peter & Paul, Wakefield

'It may well be necessary to do violence to the architectural character of the domus ecclesiae in order to build up the ecclesia, the spiritual house constructed of living stones, which gives the building its meaning and purpose.'

Peter Hammond, *Liturgy and Architecture*, p. 139

(c) Simplicity

Designing or redesigning a worship space is very like the old advice for a teaching sermon:

tell them what you are going to say
tell them
tell them you've told them
tell them again.

The community of faith needs first to consider carefully what particular emphasis within the Christian story it wishes to proclaim every time it meets. Having decided this, it needs to prepare a comprehensive plan of action to enable it to be thoroughly clear and consistent in everything it does; in the way it assembles, in its manner of celebrating the liturgy, in the symbols with which it reinforces all that it does in word and deed and gesture. Everything should be of a piece, so that the single overriding message the assembly wishes to articulate is heard and seen and experienced again and again.

Above all we must return to the primacy of the assembly as an icon of Christ. No matter how beautifully and carefully designed a worship space may be, it remains an empty stage until the cast has entered who will bring to life the words of the story. The worship space is the empty board on which the Christian assembly will, in the colour and dynamism of its own liturgical action, paint the face of Christ for the world today.

St Etienne de Froidmont, Rixensart, Belgium

For this reason many of the most splendid new places of liturgical assembly appear to us as a bare shell awaiting the entrance of the priestly community. Again, St Procopius Abbey, Illinois – considered by many to be the paradigm of the new liturgical space – shows us the way with an interior of stark simplicity devoid of ornamentation. No cross or other Christian symbol adorn the cliff-like interior walls of bare common brick. The only cross is the processional cross carried in at the beginning of the eucharist and placed near the altar; the community is the icon.

'The abbey needs no symbols. Its religious values are apparent in faithfulness to site and simple materials: in direct design, and in careful craftsmanship.'

M. W. Newman, *The Architectural Forum*, December 1972, p. 40

'A religious complex endowed with inspired simplicity, devoid of mannerism, yet rich in meaning.'

Citation of the American Institute of Architects on the Honor Award to Loebl Schlossman Bennet & Dart for their design for St Procopius Abbey

St Procopius' Abbey Church, Illinois *Photo: Michael Komechak*

'All of us want to be witnesses once more of the primitive symbols; we want to hear the primitive text, if possible without commentary. For far too long our sensibility has been the prisoner of those charming little lateral chapels; it has lost itself among all those secondary figures, among that crowded gallery of Gothic, flamboyant and baroque "commentaries". In our world of today, it is a communal home which is demanded for the people of God. Also demanded is an inspired and coherent liturgy, offered with perfect, almost drastic clarity.'

Keerprunt der Middeleeuwen 1950, quoted Debuyst, p. 29

'The worship area is simple and unadorned with excessive decoration, which would conflict with the fundamental acts of worship.' (St Procopius Abbey Church)

Charles King, *Monasticism in the Twentieth Century*, p. 19

Such buildings demonstrate powerfully the 'drastic clarity' demanded of Christians as we seek to give architectural and liturgical expression to our identity and our journey.

Monastere St Andre de Clerlande, Belgium

Such drastic clarity in the design of liturgical space is not a fashion of the moment concerned only with aesthetics, but an essential and universal prerequisite of authentic liturgy. Such simplicity sets the stage for the liturgical action in such a way as to inform and engage without obscuring or over-embellishing. It reminds us that 'the play's the thing'.

(d) Flexibility

'Flexibility' can be a dirty word for anyone who has ever worshipped in a 1960s dual-purpose building and spent every Saturday night shifting everything that moved in readiness for the Sunday eucharist. It will be touch and go whether they escaped without incurring permanent liturgical brain damage. That being said, flexibility is an important element in liturgical design today not because it enables us to play dual-purpose churches (hopefully those days are over) but because it expresses a spirituality appropriate to our age and culture.

Triumphalism, and the monumental architecture that went with it, would be totally out of place in the Church of today. Neither its current role in society, nor its current liturgical approach, allow the Church the self-indulgence of rigid formulae. There is need now to travel light, to bend, to be unpretentious, to be generous in hospitality and in the interpretation of rules, and never to think we have all the answers.

All these values can be expressed in a liturgical space which is empty of sacred objects and no-go areas, but fully available to a community of faith rediscovering in a spirit of humble enquiry the source of its life. This means a space which is flexible, and which allows the community full rein in its experimenting and evolving.

'The only fixed element in the sanctuary is the low clergy bench, built against the rear wall. The altar table, ambo and president's chair, all of heavy oak, simple and direct in construction, are movable . . . this avoids a rigidity and overly hierarchical ordering . . . and makes possible a creative flexibility in celebrating the still-evolving liturgy.' (St Procopius Abbey)

Howard Niebling, *Monastic Churches*, p. 308

Liturgical space cleared for alternative worship: St Thomas', Huddersfield

Reflection: Does our own community's liturgical space help us to understand who we are and what we are about every time we enter it and use it?

Exercise: Walk round the your own house of the church, identifying points of clutter and duplication or of lack of simplicity and clarity. Discuss how the didactic role of the building's layout and design might be made more effective.

Elements of re-ordering (3)

MOVEMENT

'Liturgical movement is an important element in stressing the involvement and participation of the whole congregation.'

Johnson & Johnson, *Planning for Liturgy*, p. 40

'As one approaches and enters the building and in turn circulates through the spaces within it, he should sense a constant change of space . . . and as one proceeds through the building, the sensation of following the patch of such a closing coil is readily noticeable. Although there are no curved surfaces, one still has the sensation of travelling along the path of a volute.'

Charles King, *Monasticism in the Twentieth Century*, p. 22

Movement is a vital element both in renewed liturgy and in the architectural treatment of the space which houses it. Movement both recalls us to our nomadic roots as God's journeying people (see chapter 6) and helps us in a practical way to involve all those present at worship to participate in the liturgical action.

Edward Dart, the architect of St Procopius Abbey, Illinois, conceived the abbey as a volute, or closing coil, in which the visitor is drawn ever closer to the heart of the community's life and work as he progresses through the various spaces within the building. St Procopius could never be described as a static building, for its architecture elicits response and demands movement, and thereby both facilitates and mirrors the liturgical action at the heart of the Abbey's life.

Two more examples illustrate how the basic principle of liturgical movement can be worked out effectively on a small as well as a grand scale.

First, the house of the Missionaries of S.Francis Xavier on Hyde Park Boulevard, Chicago, a centre established by that Order for young seminarians from Central America studying at the University of Chicago. The third floor of this four storey building (formerly a private house) is set aside for worship, and uses three rooms, separated by open archways, as three distinct liturgical spaces.

House of Xavierian
Missionaries, Chicago: Word

: Sacrament

Abbaye de Fleury, S.Benoit
sur Loire

The eucharist begins each morning in the largest of the rooms, where chairs are set out in a circle before a table on which stands the open scriptures beneath a crucifix on the wall. In this room, the community hears the call to repentance, prepares itself to approach the Lord, and listens to the Word of God. Afterwards the presider 'breaks open' the scriptures, and invites the insights and prayers of the community. After the prayers of the faithful, the community stands and moves into the second liturgical space in the adjoining room. Here there is only one item of furniture – the altar table – around which the community stands to offer the gifts, to pray the eucharistic prayer, and to administer to one another Holy Communion. Immediately after the dismissal the community disperses to its daily tasks. The third room provides the remaining liturgical space, where the Blessed Sacrament is reserved, and where individuals can pray privately.

The second picture is from France, and the XI century Benedictine Abbaye de Fleury at St Benoit sur Loire. The monastic life was restored to this ancient basilica in 1944 after a gap lasting since the Revolution, and each year at their dedication festival the monks celebrate this restoration by singing vespers on the march.

They begin outside in the magnificent arcaded 'porterie' and then enter the Abbey, singing different sections of the office in different parts of the church, ending up before the shrine of S.Benedict at the east end.

Other pictures which tell the same story of movement in worship will be familiar to most of us – for example a Palm Sunday procession which begins in a separate building to enable us to process to the place where the eucharist will be celebrated.

The re-ordered Portsmouth Cathedral shows how a house of the church can be remodelled on the theme of journey. A previously confused building was reorganised into a progression of spaces each with their own liturgical purpose. It is a paradigm of the liturgical journey.

In every case the same principle is at work; to build into our worship an element of movement which will serve to remind us that we are a pilgrim people, dwellers in tents, 'wandering Arameans' like our father Abraham.

(re St Paul, Bow Common): 'The church may be seen as a pattern of relationships, which are significant because of their function in the context of an actual liturgy; a liturgy seen as movement towards the place of altar and communion, a movement towards the light.'

Robert Maguire and Keith Murray, *Modern Churches of the World*, p. 90

St Paul, Bow Common

Too often however, we allow movement on special occasions only, and in the stultified form of a solemn procession going nowhere in particular. Normally we are content to remain stationary, in a stance which speaks of passivity.

'For my part, I travel not to go anywhere, but to go. I travel for travel's sake. The great affair is to move'.

Robert Louis Stevenson, *Travels With a Donkey*

Movement in a liturgical sense is a quite different matter, involving the whole assembly moving together from one liturgical act to another. This essential element of movement in liturgy, engaged in week by week, can be a powerful symbol of our life-long journey of faith. Movement is the hallmark of a community which knows it has not arrived, but is in transit, discovering God not at the end of the journey but in the journeying. We move because we must.

'The longest journey is the journey inwards.'

Dag Hammarskjold

And our liturgical journey reflects the journey that each of us must make to the very heart of our being.

How might we incorporate the element of movement into our regular worship by the design of our place of assembly? Here are some ideas, not all of which require alterations to the building, but all of which will help get movement into our liturgical bloodstream:

(1) Create a gathering place outside the place of assembly large enough to enable all those taking part to assemble for an introductory rite before processing into the main worship area. Such a gathering place could be used for example for the blessing of candles on the Feast of the Presentation, or of palms on Palm Sunday, for the Easter Vigil or for any occasion when there is need to pause and consider a special theme before entering the place of eucharistic assembly. The same area could double up as a narthex in which the assembly can socialise afterwards.

(2) Create a distinct area for baptism and other rites of initiation (e.g. admission to the catechumenate) which can also be used regularly at the eucharist as the place of penitence and the recalling of our baptismal vows (as well as their renewal at the Easter Vigil).

'Water in baptism signals the end of an old way of existing and the beginning of life in a new community whose vision is eternity. When we enter the church building on Sunday and consciously dip our hand into the baptismal water, we embrace this transformation again and again.'

Regina Kuehn, *A Place for Baptism*, p. 7

This area should be near the entrance into the assembly area to signify the importance of baptism as the sacrament by which we are admitted into the priestly community. The font should always remain full to the brim, and the blessed water used lavishly and as often as possible. Members of the community should be encouraged to touch the water every time they enter the assembly, and to sign themselves with the cross imprinted upon them at their baptism.

The assembly could begin the eucharist standing around the font for the penitential rite before proceeding to their places to hear the Word of God. After the absolution (preferably the conditional form) the community could file past the font to be sprinkled with water from the font as a sign of the washing away of sins in Christ.

At St Gregory of Nyssa, San Francisco, the community dances its way at the offertory from one space to the other.

(3) Create two distinct spaces for word and sacrament, enabling the assembly to move physically from one to the other at the offertory*. These two areas need not be the same size. The area for the breaking open of the Word requires seating, and space to do things differently from time to time, and to make presentations of different kinds (e.g. drama).

Because the community stands around the altar table for the eucharistic prayer and communion, the area for the breaking of the bread should not include any seating apart from a limited amount for the elderly or infirm.

In a traditional building therefore, the nave (cleared of pews) could provide a suitable space for the breaking open of the Word, and the chancel (provided it is clear of choir stalls and other clutter and the altar table placed in the centre) an equally suitable space for the breaking of the bread. Here is an opportunity for the church in rural areas to show us the way. When it comes to incorporating movement into liturgy, country churches will usually have the advantage of smaller numbers and of buildings which were originally conceived as a series of relatively separate spaces.

After communion, the community might disperse immediately to its worldly tasks (or at least as far as coffee in the gathering place), or it might return to the seating in the area of the Word for a period of silence before the notices (which are best at the end) and the dismissal. After all, after a meal at home, coffee is often taken in the living room.

Houghton S.Giles, Norfolk

Such movement is more difficult (though not impossible) when dealing with very large numbers, but is an example of where the rural church might lead the way, especially where an existing rood screen already provides the necessary two liturgical 'rooms' required.

For larger church communities, it may well be that a start could be made with smaller numbers during the week, and lessons learnt for application to Sunday worship in due course.

In all the ideas suggested above, it is important to remember that 'creating a space' does not necessarily involve the construction of walls to create separate rooms.

Certainly the gathering space needs to be a separate room because the noise of welcoming and socialising needs to be removed from the place of assembly for prayer. The other spaces mentioned above can however be demarcated in a number of different ways; by changes in floor covering or colour of carpet; by screens; by banners hanging from the ceiling; by low walls; or slight differences in level.

The creating of different spaces to enable the community to move from one part of the liturgy to another is primarily a liturgical rather than an architectural matter, and can even be done in one room. Therefore it does not necessarily cost money, indeed as we have noted, many traditional buildings already have the spaces if only they will clear them of clutter and open them up for use. What matters is the prior commitment of the community to ensure that every time they worship together they *move*. Re-pitching the tent becomes thereby integral to worship.

Reflection: In what ways might our existing place of assembly be rearranged to introduce more movement into our community's liturgy?

Exercise: plan in detail a eucharistic liturgy for a small group of a dozen or so, incorporating the element of movement as much as possible. As you plan it, walk it through in the building as you discuss each section. Consult your ordained leader to see how soon this liturgy in movement might be celebrated in your church community, as a means of involving others in the insights you are discovering.

Font Canopy, South Wigston, Leicester, by Juliet Hemingray. But will somebody *please* remove the cover!

17

Elements of re-ordering (4)

SACRIFICE

Lest we begin to run away with the idea that a buildings strategy is all to do with worship or all to do with ourselves, the theme of sacrifice will bring us to our senses.

'You say, "How have we despised thy name?" By offering polluted food upon my altar . . . by thinking that the Lord's table may be despised. When you offer blind animals in sacrifice, is that no evil? And when you offer those that are lame or sick, is that no evil?

Malachi 1.6–8

Sacrifice can be understood firstly in terms of costly sacrificial worship, of giving of our very best to God. In this, the warnings of the prophets against presenting shoddy goods at the altar is all too timely. Our generation has grown into bad habits whereby it appears that, where the Church is concerned, anything goes; dirty purificators on the altar, and foreign coins on the plate.

'And this is the offering you shall receive from them: gold, silver, and bronze, blue and purple and scarlet stuff and fine twined linen, goats' hair, tanned rams' skins, goatskins, acacia wood, oil for the lamps, spices for the anointing oil and for the fragrant incense, onyx stones and stones for setting, for the ephod and for the breastpiece. And

Our reordering needs to involve sacrificial generosity of space, time, talents and wealth, if we are to make something beautiful for God in our own era. Only the very best will do.

St John Baptist, Hove. *Photo: Stefano Cagnoni*

'Let them make me a
sanctuary, that I may dwell
in their midst.'

Exodus 25.3–5

'Truly, I say to you, as you
did it to one of the least of
these my brethren, you did
it to me.'

Matthew 25.40

Sacrifice can be understood secondly in terms of Jesus laying down his life for his friends (John 15.13) and our buildings need to be part of the deal. In so far as we open them up, share them and place them at the disposal of others, our buildings will be signs of the Kingdom, of God's reckless generosity given concrete expression through his faithful people.

So far we have been dealing almost exclusively with the re-ordering of the place of liturgical assembly as a means of revitalising the community of faith at worship. From the pages of the gospels we get a clear picture of Jesus as someone who was highly critical of religiosity; a right relationship with God had to spill over into our relationship with neighbour.

'If the Church is seriously
concerned to engage with
and live out the Gospel,
then its buildings should
reflect the accessibility of
Jesus.

Peter Cavanagh, *Church
Buildings* p. 4

We now need to examine therefore the potential of buildings as aids to the Christian community in implementing the social teaching of Jesus. This is not an alternative to a strong liturgical life, but a fruit of it.

It is often from very little acorns that great oaks of community projects grow. It may even start with something as prosaic as a lavatory. After years of embarrassment, directing cross-legged visitors to the nearest hedge or to the pub across the road, the cry goes up 'it's time we had a loo in the place'.

This is no bad thing, for it reveals a concern to be better hosts than previously, and usually leads to the installation of kitchen facilities also, before very long. There may be a long way to go from the installation of a loo to the opening of a night shelter for the homeless, but the simple desire to be hospitable is a good starting point.

Sikh gurdwara, Huddersfield:

. . . upstairs

. . . downstairs

'The adaption of churches to serve also as, for example, halls and/or community centres is an opportunity for the Church to serve the community.'

Faith in the City, p. 12

As so often is the case, our relations in faith from other branches of Abraham's family put us to shame. The Sikh gurdwara in Huddersfield has the whole ground floor given over to cooking and catering, with worship facilities upstairs; the sacred space rests physically on the kitchen. In this respect the Sikhs show the Christians (we who are supposed to be above all a table fellowship) the way, recalling us to our own tradition.

In England, 1995 saw the 10th anniversary of the Faith in the City report, which led to the setting up of the Church Urban Fund to assist Anglican parishes in urban areas of social deprivation. CUF has given a real shot in the arm to the Christian presence in key locations in our cities, enabling our worshipping communities to rediscover their holy Christian tradition in which love of God and love of neighbour is inextricably bound together. In 1996 alone, the Fund made available grants totalling £3.1 million.

In 1995, CUF inaugurated the Keystones Competition – a unique initiative to highlight the imaginative work going on throughout the country to refurbish church buildings and restore them to a central role in the communities they serve.

Recalled to our spiritual roots in this way, the worshipping community needs to ensure that its design strategy makes integral to its buildings a number of interrelated uses and activities of which worship will be but one element, albeit of overriding importance. In this we recall the buildings complex of the early Christian Church in which the basilica was but one component (see chapter 8).

Using its Mission Statement and Buildings Strategy as starting points, the community needs to determine a design approach for the whole complex so that it may speak to the passer-by of a community which is willing to lay down its life for its friends.

A new entrance – bright, attractive, well-lit, easily accessible to all, and with a dash of high-tech to spice it

Dewsbury Minster

The Cotteridge Church,
Birmingham

Approach to a parish office,
Hertfordshire

up a little – can transform the way in which a building, even a tired old building, is perceived. In the same way that the receptionist is the most important person in the hierarchy of a commercial firm (if she's grumpy or inefficient you can close the order books now) so the entrance is the key to evangelisation through the built environment. The entrance to our house of the church – the way in to the community's worship, its hospitality, its bandaging of the wounds of life – needs to catch the eye of those most in need of God's love, for whatever reason. It needs to be bright eyed and bushy tailed, to be accessible to all and to say 'welcome'!

Part of the secret of unlocking our buildings – literally as well as figuratively – is to employ devices which will ensure that people are coming in and out of them all day, that there is something going on there, that the coffee is always on the boil.

The parish community should move heaven and earth to establish within the building uses which generate activity, which give people reasons to come in and out throughout the working day, and excuses to pop into the place of assembly for a moment of prayer. In other words, the building becomes the community's operational HQ, instead of a deserted (and usually bolted) mausoleum Monday to Saturday.

The basic ingredient in this approach is the establishment of a welcome desk at the main entrance, manned by a couple of (smiling!) members of the community of faith, who will be the community's first contact with anyone who walks through the door or calls by telephone. It will also help if the parish office is located in the same building that contains the worship area (and maybe also the ordained team leader's office), but this should only be contemplated as part of an overall and well-integrated plan for the building. It is not a bit of good having a parish office round the back in an old vestry which the intrepid visitor approaches through long wet grass and across slippery stone flags forever egged on by signs reading 'use other door'.

The temptation to use back door solutions must always be resisted. It is easy to put the problem people 'down in the crypt' while the community of faith gets on with the worship upstairs, hardly affected by their presence until they read the annual accounts. At all costs a single point of entry must be established to all the various activities which the community of faith is called upon to do in obedience to its Master, whether in breaking of the bread or binding up the broken hearted. It is all one work, a fact of which the layout of the building needs to remind us – and those we serve – every time we enter the house of the church.

A community of faith whose will has completely re-aligned itself vis-à-vis its neighbourhood is St Augustine Bradford, where under the leadership of Robin Gamble, a Victorian fortress-mausoleum was torn apart to be re-built as a paradigm of the house of the church which looks outward to those around. The reconstructed building is itself a parable of the Risen Christ, in that it is recognisable (just about!) as the building people remember, but is completely transformed and irradiated with God's life and vigour.

St Augustine Bradford
(Ashfield Architects, York)

At St Augustine's the visitor enters through a gathering place which is all glass and steelwork in primary colours, to discover a restaurant where an ethnic mix of people are enjoying good food in attractive surroundings, while others thread their way through the

'All guests . . . shall be received as Christ himself: for he will one day say "I was a stranger, and you took me in".'

Rule of St Benedict, 53.

tables en route to the City Council's branch library also established within the building. All who come and go can look through into, and enter freely, the magnificent new area of liturgical assembly of the servants of Jesus whose commands are being carried out in and from this building seven days a week.

In the English situation, it is important to remember that it is the element of community service in our re-ordering schemes that will unlock funding from secular as well as religious charitable trusts. We have a whole host of friends out there ready to assist us once they see that the Church itself means business.

'but they who wait for the Lord shall renew their strength, they shall mount up with wings like eagles, they shall run and not be weary, they shall walk and not faint.'

Isaiah 40.31

Experience shows that renewal of the building, and enlargement thereby of its capacity for hospitality and service, has led to the renewal of the worshipping community in that place, and to growth in numbers as well as in maturity of faith.

Reflection: How can our community develop, and hold in unity, a greater variety of activities in love of God and neighbour, and how can our building help us carry out this mission?

Exercise: Identify the most urgent social needs in the area where you live, using the help of the appropriate department of your local civil authority to direct you to real needs rather than perceived or remembered ones. What potential capacity does your building have to help meet these needs, and how might that capacity be made the most of?

Our mobilisation

18

Once a Christian community has begun to realise its true and unique identity under God, once we know who we really are, how can the whole body of the local church be stirred to act upon these discoveries and developments?

If we are going to attempt to make the 'house of the church' a real home for the community of faith; if it is to be the setting for a missionary congregation's exploration and encounter in prayer, and worship and service, then we are talking about more than just making room for a nave altar and putting a loo under the tower. We are talking revolution.

'A missionary congregation is a church which takes its identity, priorities, and agenda, from participation in God's mission in the world.'

Robert Warren, *Building Missionary Congregations*, p. 4

We are dealing with a spiritual process, which we might call liturgical formation, in which a community of faith discovers its identity and vocation under God and determines how to express those characteristics in the physical environment of its worship and work.

'Britain has opted for a comfortable society, rather than an achieving one. It wants modernisation of comforts, with the old institutions unchanged.'

'Analysis', BBC Radio 4, 4 April 1991

The reality of course is frequently very different. A great many of our parishes have embraced what J. K. Galbraith has called 'the culture of contentment'. Given the prevailing norms of British culture, that is hardly surprising.

Significantly, the common perception of an unfaithful leadership is all to do with failure to keep people

'. . . our spiritual leaders were more interested in protecting their institutions than in understanding the mystery that symbols present'.

Carl G. Jung (ed.), *Man and his Symbols*

'Change is the game today, and organisations that can't deal with it effectively aren't likely to be around long.'

William Bridges, *Managing Transitions*, p. ix

'When Christ calls a person, he bids them come and die.'

Dietrich Bonhoeffer, *The Cost of Discipleship*

'In this situation, it is a matter of the conversion of a community rather than an individual. It involves the turning around of a whole group to face the mission implications of being Christian. Such change is essentially both simple and costly.'

Robert Warren, *Building Missionary Congregations*, p. 33

happy, rather than failure to proclaim and to be good news. Anglican clergy in particular are haunted by the fear of 'losing people', whereas some selective early pruning is exactly what's needed to promote vigorous growth.

We are dealing here with the management of change, and nothing can be more difficult in the life of a parish community nor more daunting to the ordained leadership. Those with the care of all the churches (unless arriving with experience of the big bad world in a previous existence) come to the parochial front line completely unprepared for the task.

No one has warned them just how vicious people can become when their precious church-museum is threatened with 'desecration', and all too often it takes only a poison-pen letter (with a copy to the bishop!) to ensure a sudden loss of enthusiasm by the clergy. There is little awareness of the basic fact of life that change, and therefore discipleship, is costly.

In England, the absence of the management of change from the syllabuses of our theological colleges is symptomatic of the 'English disease'. Not only is change not prepared for, it is not expected.

Liturgical formation is either confined to the narrow consideration of liturgical texts or is ignored altogether. Because the Church doesn't expect change, it sees no need to prepare for it or to equip its leadership to make it happen. The public lavatory syndrome rules OK – that we leave a parish in the same state as we found it; there is zero expectation that we should put in new plumbing, upgrade the whole facility or even relocate it.

'Renovating a church . . . is about translating a liturgical theology and beauty into three dimensions. It is about forming a holy people whose lives are transformed, motivated, formed, and sustained by their experiences in that place.'

Marchita Mauck, *Places for Worship*, p. 7

The engagement of the whole community is therefore crucial from the outset, and it is necessary to approach the whole project in a sense of expectation rather than dread. There is no need for long faces and worried frowns; we are on our way to the building committee meeting, not to our own execution. No one must talk us out of our conviction that to redesign liturgical space is an exciting and rewarding enterprise in which we are drawn closer to the mystery of God and his purpose for us. Above all, it can actually be fun.

We need to consider ways in which every member of the assembly can be mobilised to ensure that no one is excluded and that any final proposals have the widest possible support. This process might be divided into two basic stages; catching the vision and sharing the vision.

(a) Catching the vision. It is a very tall order indeed to imagine that, overnight, a whole parish community is going to come to a common mind on something as tricky as the radical alteration of the house of the church.

The Scriptural pattern is that a lone prophetic voice speaks the vision of God, and that via an inner circle of close associates, the vision spreads in ever widening circles until it embraces the whole people. This may take time (it took Moses a lifetime!) but the progression is a natural one familiar to us from many walks of life.

So it is good sense always to begin with a small working group. Ideas involving change usually begin with a 'crazy dreamer' and rarely have immediate appeal to a wider audience. Such ideas need careful nurture in the greenhouse before being exposed to the elements out in the allotment.

This is partly because new ideas are not always easy to articulate clearly, especially at the preliminary stage when even the dreamer has only a day-dream, a hunch, rather than a blue-print. He or she may have very little idea at that stage as to the ramifications of the day-dream, and the small group will play a vital part in testing the ideas and working out the next step. Furthermore, half-formed ideas appropriate for kicking around in a small group can spread panic if tossed too soon into the larger pool.

Certainly it seems to have been the method employed by Jesus to begin with an inner circle and to work outwards. Even within the Twelve, he confided first in the inner core of three, Peter, James and John, who alone were party to significant moments in their leader's life e.g. the Transfiguration.

In a parish context, the working group might consist of the ordained leader's staff meeting or simply two or three trusted lieutenants. Alternatively (for we must not assume that it is the ordained leader who will be the visionary) the small group might be one nominated by the leader and the church council to look into this whole question and report back.

The task of the group will be to explore and experiment:

- to explore what other Christian communities are doing, and to return to base excited about what they have seen and positive about how good practice might be applied at home.
- to suggest and to organise experiments in the use of the building to help others glimpse the vision. This may involve changes to seating plan, to running order, or to musical accompaniment. It may even involve a temporary move to other premises – always a good catalyst of liturgical renewal. The details are less important than the overriding need to inculcate a climate of change in which the dynamic becomes natural and the static abnormal.

(b) Sharing the vision. From the outset, the body which sets up the working group (the PCC or equivalent), should be careful to give it clearly defined terms of reference, together with a timetable and an overall framework into which the working group's findings can be fitted.

In this way, the vision of the working group, if adopted by its parent body, can begin to be presented to and shared with an ever-widening circle of participants, through a series of well-defined and clearly-timetabled stages.

In an Anglican setting, these circles of participation will involve Parochial Church Council, Diocesan Advisory Committee, Sunday congregation, Electoral Roll membership, local community, as well as in some cases the Council for the Care of Churches and the amenity societies.

A suggested detailed framework of consultation is set out in Appendix A.

Reflection:

1. Does our church community accept the basic need for change as part of living the gospel?

2. As a sign of inner conversion, how important is it for our community to change the physical structure of what we see and handle every time the Christian assembly meets?

Exercise:

1. From what quarter in your own community is opposition to change likely to come?

2. Can the underlying reasons for such opposition be discerned, and if so, in what ways might they be brought out into the open and discussed constructively?

3. How far should our church community go down the road of compromise? What should be our sticking point? Is there a price to pay for doing nothing? Are we ready to face legal action?

PART THREE:

Where are we going?

(A liturgical design guide)

St Charles Borromeo, Ogle St, London

Introduction

'Apart from the community it serves, the church edifice has no meaning.'

Kevin Seasoltz, *The House of God: Sacred Art and Church Architecture*

Having considered the built environment of worship, the house of the church, in history and in our own strategic thinking, the time has now come to lay hands on a few sticks and stones. As God's artists we have thought our great thoughts and the awful moment has now arrived when we must make the first mark on the beautiful and untouched sheet of white paper. We hesitate, we walk around the room, and pour ourselves another cup of coffee.

This is the most difficult part of the process, for three reasons. Firstly we are above all designing for mystery, for something beyond that which we can contrive or control. Frederic Debuyst describes the Christian church building as nothing more or less than 'a Paschal meeting room', a place for engaging in the Mystery of what it means for an Easter people to gather and celebrate the presence of the Risen Lord Christ standing among them.

'The Christian church is neither a sacred monument built to express God's glory, nor a simple gathering centre for biblical lectures or social proceedings. It is a Paschal meeting-room, a place where the assembled community experiments and exercises the full impact of the Paschal Mystery.'

Frederic Debuyst, *Modern Architecture & Christian Celebration*, p. 20

The Cistercian genius, Pontigny Abbey

In such a task there can be no unfailing mechanisms for producing the desired effect, for we stand on holy ground. Each liturgical space is a particular response of a local community of faith unique in God's sight.

This in turn means that in liturgical design we are not primarily concerned with designing a series of 'objects' (font, ambo altar etc), but with creating a space in which the 'subject' (the assembly itself) can give full and deep expression to its life in the Risen Christ.

Here, the Christian community has much to learn from the theatre, for the stage designer is in all but name a designer of liturgical space. The stage designer sets the scene, creates the space, in which the written text of the play is brought to life, and the audience transported to another world, even carried to another plane of existence. The detailed design of the stage will have a tremendous impact on how the players interpret the play, and to what extent the audience is caught up in the action. Above all the stage designer is the master of space.

Stage set for The Crucible by Arthur Miller: 'A design inspired by the line "space so antagonistic to man". The play gave out a strong fear of space, the wilderness at the edge of "strict order".'

Kandis Cook

The Imagination Centre

In Christian liturgy we go a step further, for there is no audience, only participants in the unfolding drama of the saving work of Jesus of Nazareth, the Christ.

We restrict ourselves all too readily, however, to the ground floor, clamped and confined in a two-dimensional approach. The one asset possessed to excess by the vast majority of our church buildings is height and volume; how little we use them for dramatic effect. The walkways high in the atrium of the Imagination Building in London, for example, are the very feature which make this space an exciting space for theatre; the excess of height over width is a problem turned into a celebration.

'In the religion of the temple, sacrality ("the sacred") affected the cultic objects and the architectural symbols as such, directly. In the Christian faith, on the contrary, sacrality does not affect anything directly, except the celebration itself, and the persons celebrating. We must even say that Christian sacrality has no real "object". It has only a "subject": the risen Christ, present in the eucharist in the Communion of the assembled Church.'

Frederic Debuyst, *Modern Architecture & Christian Celebration*, p. 23

'In a church renovation or construction project, the process is as important as the product only if one believes in the incarnation, in the reality that the spiritual is embodied in the physical. Building a church of brick and board is the efficacious sign, the sacrament, of the building of a church of blood and breath.'

David Philippart, *Environment and Art Newsletter*, March 1995, Archdiocese of Chicago

At the same time, the theatre reminds us too that the performance is everything. No matter how inspirational the set, it is the actors and they alone, who can bring the play to life. The set may excite our imagination, but only the players can transfix us and carry us away to new worlds. This echoes the insight of the Christian New Covenant in which the biblical concept of temple is transposed from building materials of stone and timber to human materials of hearts and minds.

At the heart of Christian worship therefore lies the mystery of the transformation of the people of God themselves into temples of the Holy Spirit, and the task of transferring this truth to the drawing board is not an easy one.

Although mystery will remain by definition an elusive element in the design of liturgical space, nevertheless it is possible to develop skills in the formation of space, the use of light and the design of detail, which will help recall us constantly to the unknowable in the midst of the tangible.

St Martin, London E13 (Cottrell and Vermeuler). Photo: Paul Ratigan.

*Although St Jude's Peterborough is a striking new house of the Church (completed 1984), for me the very best liturgical space in that parish was actually the kitchen in the home of a family in our parish community. It was a delightful top-lit white-walled space with quarry tiled floor, a warm intimate room where hospitality abounded and where people could be themselves. It was a space I always wanted to make eucharist in; it was a good liturgical space because it was a good human space.

Secondly, we have been conditioned by post-Constantinian Christian thought into seeing the church building as a monument when what we need is a home. Drawing upon the Church's invigorating experience in the domestic era of its development, we need to create in our buildings genuinely human space.*

Like the house-churches of the early centuries, our buildings should provide us houses which can become homes for the Christian assembly, showing us how to be fully human in order that we may become more fully church.

We need today, not buildings that make grandiose or pretentious statements, but buildings that make us feel at home.

St John, Newsome, Huddersfield

'God lurks in the detail.'
Aby Warburg, founder of the
Warburg Institute

'The Scottish architect
Charles Rennie
Mackintosh showed how
things as mundane and
inexpensive as a chair, a
window or a pane of glass
could be glorious works of
art – at the same time
inspiring and functional.'
Peter Cavanagh, *Church
Buildings*, p. 2

'We can do no great things
– only small things with
great love.'
Mother Teresa

Thirdly, we are all too well aware of glaring errors in buildings familiar to us, of our design or rank insensitivity which has marred an otherwise outstanding place of worship. It might take only the wrong choice of carpet to write off, in visual terms, a re-ordering scheme which has taken years and cost the earth. There is indeed many a liturgical ship spoilt for just a ha'peth of tar.

It is right that we hesitate, but there is no need for us to render ourselves incapable of action. Inspired design is a gift, and good taste a very subjective affair, but nevertheless it is possible for us all, without exception, to train ourselves to observe, to compare and to appreciate, so that we become adept at knowing quality when we see it, and sensing special atmosphere when we enter it. We shall also get better at spotting what is inappropriate or just plain cheap and nasty, and analysing why some of the Church's buildings just don't make it as inspiring and creative places of Christian assembly. It is perfectly possible to learn good practice.

To help in this task of getting the detail right, the following nine chapters tackle one by one the constituent parts of the house of the Church giving detailed guidance on how each area might be designed or redesigned in the light of the principles and strategies outlined earlier.

These should be read in conjunction with the appendices dealing with particular elements of detailed design (e.g. lighting) relevant to all areas of the building.

Finally, we all know that a camel is a horse designed by a committee, so beware! Committees are not appropriate bodies for carrying out detailed design, and the worshipping community needs to discern the gifts of those with this particular expertise and, having set the guidelines and the financial constraints, allow them to get on with it.

Didsbury, Manchester; Nick Rank

19 Presenting the building

The approach to the building is all important. First impressions may for the visitor make the difference between closer inspection and turning on one's heels and running for one's life.

The Christian community needs to learn how to present its buildings well, remembering that in this subject, presentation gets as high a mark as content. Without good presentation, the contents will never be experienced by the vast majority of the population who have already dismissed the Church as peripheral to real life.

(a) Approach

Previous generations of Christians went to great lengths to announce the house of the church in such a way as to dominate the landscape, and if we have inherited such an advantage, we should enhance their work with everything that modern technology or contemporary design expertise can muster.

On the other hand, if dominating the landscape is crippling our community (through the financial burden of maintaining a spire for example) it may be too high a price to pay.

The demands of the community's Mission Statement should always recall it to its true priorities.

Despite the dire warnings found in Luke 14.28–30, tower building is not a completely dead art in the Church today.

St Jude, Peterborough

At St Jude, Peterborough the community of faith had been camping out in a half-completed and character-less dual purpose building for 20 years, and when a permanent house of the church was completed in 1984 it seemed a good idea to present the new building in such a way that no one would be left in any doubt in that (very flat) neighbourhood that the Church had arrived in earnest. The impact of the tower was heightened by floodlighting and by the installation of three bells from a redundant building which were rung Continental fashion (much to the annoyance of the neighbours).

By way of contrast, the nearby parish of Eye, Peterborough, was at the same time moving in the opposite direction, dismantling its very fine spire, because it was no longer an affordable luxury, and putting a superbly designed pitched roof on what remained of the tower. Here were two quite different solutions, equally valid.

(b) Making the most of what we have

Like a lady who has reached the age when she would rather forget her birthdays, our building needs to present itself in such a way that the good points are emphasized and the not-so-good disguised. St Edmund Forest Gate is a community which really does meet in a house (the former Vicarage), and the 1994 refurbishment scheme skilfully drew attention away from the rather nondescript appearance of the building, with a new construction coming right up to the edge of the pavement, which catches the eye and stimulates the imagination. The boundary wall of the exterior liturgical space (used for lighting the Easter fire for example) doubles up as a bench seat for the bus stop immediately outside the front door. There is something deeply theological about this couple of metres of low brick wall with stone capping. It provides (depending on which way round one sits) both liturgical seating and a resting place for weary travellers. The Church's dual role could not be more nicely expressed.

St Edmund Forest Gate

(c) Exterior condition

Whatever the shape of our building, we must ensure that when people come for a closer look at our home they are not repelled by dirt behind the ears; our buildings should sparkle in the sun. Never mind the gloomy prognostications of the 'expert' who can always be found to pontificate on the dangers of stone cleaning; anyone who has ever experienced such a scheme first-hand will testify to the amazing transformation achieved thereby in the public's perception of the building and of the community that worships there. A building blackened by a century or more of industrial pollution is often assumed to have closed down. Once stone-cleaned however, it is suddenly recognisable as a house of the Church again, usually amidst widespread surprise and pleasure on the part of the local population.

(d) Signing

Good signing is a vital ingredient of good presentation. This includes both signs to direct people to the building, and signs identifying it when they get there. This does not include signs telling you all the services, the pastor's name (certainly not all his degrees!) and the name of the verger's dog. *Identification* is all that is required, and all other detail can be supplied within the entrance area.

Where possible, it is a simple and effective idea to build into the structure itself the name of the community using the building, thereby making the vandal's lot a less than happy one. This can be achieved on a DIY basis by pouring cement into a timber mould around the required script spelt out in polystyrene letters (available from graphics suppliers).

In situations where a dedication or commemoration stone is required, let it be not merely a means of sharing information, but a work of art in itself. On completion of a re-ordering scheme, consult a craftsman to ensure that the building is graced for as long as

St Thomas' Huddersfield before . . .

. . . and after

St Jude Peterborough

Dedication stone,
St Thomas', Huddersfield;
Celia Kilner

Parish church, Biras,
Dordogne.
Good presentation . . .

. . . by day

. . . by night

it stands with a piece of beautifully designed calligraphy to mark this milestone in its history.

(e) Grounds

Most of our buildings sit in grounds of some kind, and, whether hard or soft, these can be turned to our advantage in improving the presentation of the building to the street.

Parishes in urban areas, with buildings surrounded by paved forecourts fenced off from the street, might demolish boundary walls to open up the forecourt to the street, bringing it into the public domain by making it part of the pavement (with luck, the local authority might design the scheme and share the cost). In this way, the building is made to look more approachable and friendly, no longer set apart and distant. The 'zone of self-consciousness' for the timid visitor is reduced or removed, a *piazza* is created on your doorstep and good theology is proclaimed.

Alternatively the churchyard can be an oasis of green which we need to repaint with a bold brush. The delight of a real churchyard is the massive scale of its tree cover, and our own generation must declare war on the planting of silly little trees and shrubs appropriate only to a tiny front garden. (See Appendix C.)

Most churchwardens (or equivalent officers) have a hard time of it keeping on top of churchyard maintenance, but this necessity can be turned to pastoral advantage by organising occasional working parties (which can be fun events if organised well) for a regular blitz on accumulations of leaves in gutters and half-eaten take-aways in the bushes. In this way can the building be presented to the passer-by as the pride and joy of an active and caring community.

Reflection: Is my church community making the most of its building to present the living Church to those who pass by?

Group Exercise: Consider the building's worst feature, or its main drawback as local centre for worship and mission. What ways can you think of to offset such disadvantages?

A possible checklist might include:
- disguise – painting (e.g. painting out any white 1960s fascia boards or ranch fencing in dark colours, or painting out any 'wood-grain effect' doors in a colour relating to stone or brickwork);
- camouflage – planting virginia creeper on severe or unattractive elevations, or Russian vine over the really hideous flat-roofed extension;
- diversion – redesigning a part of the building (with a new 'high-tech' entrance) to draw the eye;
- cleaning – check with the Local Authority about grants for stone cleaning;
- signing – devise a logo to give your premises (and your stationery) a new look;
- landscaping – be generous to the environment as the environment has been generous to you (see Appendix C);
- churchyard maintenance – provide an oasis whenever you can (see Appendix C);
- hard landscaping – is there any way in which your forecourt might be made part of the street? Discuss with your local authority the possibility of a joint scheme.

St Catherine, Sandal, Wakefield

Plymouth Cathedral

20 Entering the building

'Is this an entrance, or is it an entrance?' The porch-tower, St Benoît-sur-Loire

In England, the 1996 Disability Discrimination Act requires all public buildings to be made more user-friendly to people with disabilities.

'People wishing to engage in its activities have to cross the no-man's land of the graveyard, push open heavy doors and step out of sight of familiar surroundings, entering . . . a different world.'

Peter Cavanagh, *Church Buildings*, p. 4

The entrance, the threshold, of any building is of immense importance in determining our first impression of the household or organisation we are visiting. It is a place where we allow observation of minute detail to assume great significance as we attempt – within the space of perhaps only a few seconds – to get the feel of what we are letting ourselves in for. It is also a place of decision, of momentary hestitation, in the split second before the door opens and a new encounter is set in motion.

The entrance to the house of the church needs above all to be obvious. Places of worship seem to specialise in grandiose portals – great west doors and the like – which turn out not to be the entrance but a mere diversionary tactic, the actual entrance being the small door round the side. In this way the visitor is led up the garden path and feels a fool. The actual entrance should be quite clearly indicated at the point of entry into the church grounds, by signing, hard landscaping, and lighting. It should be wheelchair-accessible*.

In this post-Christian era it is embarrassing enough for anyone to be seen going into a church, let alone to be spotted acting suspiciously in a churchyard, trying every door in turn before gaining entry. Difficult though it is for us within the Church to understand, for those outside, our ecclesiastical world remains alien territory requiring considerable effort and courage to penetrate. Our task as Christians with a welcome to give and a story to tell, is to remove one by one every obstacle which might just conceivably deter anyone (however improbable it may seem to us) from taking a closer look at who we are and what we are doing.

The majority of our main entrances are partly enclosed by a porch of some kind, and the porch merits careful attention to ensure that the faint hearted do not turn back at this point. Open porches are now a liability in terms of loitering with all kinds of dubious intent, and should therefore be enclosed with outer doors so that the porch becomes a lobby, i.e. an interior rather than an exterior space.

As well as helping with draft exclusion, this means that the community can make the most of the porch as a place of initial welcome. In every community there lurks a member with a special gift for home-making/nest-building. The entrance to their own home will tell you all you need to know about the qualifications for this ministry. Identify them and give them a completely free hand, unmolested by any committee, to create an entrance porch – white walls, spot lights, potted plants on the window sill, carpet on the floor – which will radiate a first impression of warmth and welcome sufficient to cover the multitude of sins possibly to be encountered later.

St Mark, Harrogate;
James Thorp

Doorways of our ancient houses of the Church were often places of great significance in the proclamation of the great story which the whole building was to unfold to the worshipper or pilgrim. A tympanum above a great west door might contain a powerful representation of Christ in majesty, the columns at either side displaying the figures of the prophets and apostles upon whom the community of living stones was built; the doorway was more than an entrance it was a place of prayer.

At Santiago de Compostella, the stone of the central arch of the great west door of the cathedral has been almost worn away by the kisses of the pilgrims who, over the centuries, have been overcome with joy and thankfulness to God having arrived safely at this doorway into a sacred place.

Santiago de Compostela

Higham Ferrers, west entrance. Photo: Brian Cox

If you happen to have a medieval tympanum to play with, make the most of it, and restore it to pride of place as an entrance not just a curiosity. At Higham Ferrers, the main west entrance which contained a fine tympanum and also faced directly the main street, was obstructed by a ground floor ringing chamber, requiring all-comers to enter the building via a side entrance. In the reordering of 1969, the west entrance was restored; the bellringers were sent upstairs to a new gallery, glazed inner doors installed, and the south porch (the previous main entrance) converted into a sacristy.

If we don't happen to have a medieval masterpiece up our sleeve, let us at least try to provide something of beauty and excellence with which to entice the visitor into an encounter with God in our assembly. St Benedict the African, a new house of the Church on the wrong side of the tracks in Chicago's South Side, is an object lesson in this respect.

St Benedict the African, Chicago

A dedication stone, bearing a poignant message of great beauty, greets the visitor before he has even crossed the threshold, and as soon as he does, he is greeted by an attractive banner representing the typical (Black) family who worship in this place, and by a glimpse of an entrance area which is full of curved walls which prompt us to want to see round the corner.

Even the door itself is of great importance in giving clues to the character of the community that meets behind it. There is no reason why outer doors should be varnished with a wood grain finish; introduce some colour here (usually the only opportunity in the whole exterior facade) with a careful choice of paint to pick out colours discernible in the external stone or brick work.

Door handle, Cologne

Door handle, St Christopher,
Blackpool (Francis Roberts)

Even a door handle can make a difference! The exquisitely crafted door handles, in the shape of a fish, a feature of some of the re-ordered romanesque churches of Cologne, are a joy to look at and to touch. A delightful detail to encourage the most sceptical of seekers to go further; the pleasure of turning the handle is reward enough.

Where possible, the door from the porch into the house should be glazed, to allow the visitor to see inside before entering, and hopefully to tempt them to proceed by the excellence of what they can see. Otherwise, the click of the latch, the creaking of the door and the literal falling into the nave (especially if occupied by gawping worshippers), are common features guaranteed to deter for another year or two all but the most intrepid of seekers after truth.

Reflection: What must it be like to have to enter our building for the first time? Would it be a pleasant experience via an easy well defined route? If not, what can we do about it?

Group Exercise: Take a walk together into your own building and discuss how it might appear to a stranger. Run through the following check list and see how your entrance shapes up:

1. Is the way into your church obvious at first glance from the point where people enter your site? If unsure, arrange for another parish to do a 'consumer survey' for you to help undertand how it feels for the newcomer.

2. If a number of doors are visible from the road, ensure that signing and hard landscaping make the main entrance obvious, in order to save time and embarrassment for the visitor.

3. Do you have a special feature at your entrance point? In what ways can you highlight it and give it greater prominence?

4. What feature might you install at the entrance doorway to delight the visitor, give them some clue as to the nature of your community, and encourage them to enquire within?

5. Does the system of entrances to your building need a thorough reappraisal and rearrangement? Is there more than one entrance in use, if so, why?

6. How can we discern and use the gift of interior design and home-making, given to certain members of our community?

7. Is there any way in which the redesign/repositioning of doors can make a difference to how newcomers perceive our community?

8. What improvements are necessary to make access to our building user-friendly to those with disabilities?

Church door, island of Halki, the Dodecanese

21

The gathering place

'The first thing an assembly does is assemble: making one another welcome, taking places near the altar table and near one another. Assemblies have to assemble, to get together.'

Gabe Huck, *The Assembly Building and Renovation Kit for Places of Catholic Worship*

'Our homes also have a ritual opening or hole. It is the fireplace . . . We may not need the fireplace for its heat, but everyone appreciates its ceremonial warmth.'

Gertrud Mueller Nelson, *To Dance with God*

*In Nepali culture, the hearth is a holy place, for the household gods reside there. The seat of honour is next to the fire, and you may sit there only when invited by the host.

'Whoever does the will of God is my brother, and sister, and mother.'

Mark 3.32–35

The gathering place, or narthex, is the 'common room' of the community of faith. Indeed, in the United States this area is often referred to as the 'Commons'. In the progression of spaces encountered by the visitor to the community, it is the place of welcome and hospitality. In a way, it could be perceived as the last 'non-religious zone' before getting down to the serious business, but to think of it like that would be to intrude a false dichotomy between sacred and secular, for in giving hospitality as much as in its sacred liturgies, the community is living out its faithfulness to its Lord.

The chief purpose of the gathering place is to provide a 'hearth'* around which the community of faith can gather, relax and feel most at home. For this reason, as already noted, a fireplace (a real working one) is a frequent feature of the gathering place in houses of the church in the United States. Other features of the traditional home – a grandfather clock, photos of community members for example – are also often thrown in for good measure to repeat the message that it is when Christians gather as the assembly of God's people that they are most true to themselves, most acutely aware that they have come home to God. The truth that we have more in common with our brothers and sisters in Christ than with our blood relations is there at the heart of Jesus' teaching, shocking though it may be to our ears.

Hospitality will therefore always be the key to the successful gathering place (and we have already seen how seriously other religious communities take hospitality as integral to gatherings for worship). This means that our gathering spaces need to be built around a kitchen, and be large enough to accommodate the whole community (if they have to squeeze in, then so much the better for healing us of our fear of touch!).

Sunday coffee . . .

. . . West Yorkshire

. . . California

There are countless church communities of warm-hearted people anxious to welcome newcomers but utterly frustrated in their desire by a building which has no capacity for translating that welcome into practical hospitality. A kitchen, toilets and other ancillary services such as cloakrooms and storage space, are therefore essential in the life of a community which aspires to follow its Master in loving both God and neighbour.

It is always open season for preservationists hunting down Christians caught drinking coffee in church, but those who see our buildings as primarily architectural objects rather than houses of the church have little concept of building community. Their interest lies in dead stones, and in living stones only in so far as they keep the dead ones in good repair. If God is worshipped at all, it is a private matter to be entered into during the first hymn and terminated during the last; God forbid that eyes should meet or bodies touch.

How any Christian community survives without a gathering place with basic catering facilities is nothing short of a miracle. Moreover it needs to be a gathering place under the same roof as the place of liturgical assembly. A gathering place along the road, or even across a churchyard, might as well be on the other side of the moon for all the use it will be in helping to build community, to be church.

Unless the newcomer (not to mention the regular who claims he never has time to stop and talk) can be ushered easily from worship into fellowship, to find a cup of coffee in their hand before they can say 'Book of Common Prayer', our attempts to strengthen our community will be constantly undermined. Of course the interested and the informed will win through, but evangelisation is primarily concerned with those who won't make it on their own – with the shy, the broken, and the inadequate – who need every bit of help we can give them.

If our community's existing building does not contain a gathering place, then one must be made. If we have inherited a single-chamber building providing one vast worship space with no ancillary facilities, then we must carve one out of the space we have, even at the risk of losing seats. Like all building decisions, this should arise from a predetermined mission strategy in which nurture of the week-by-week community is likely to be given higher priority than the maintenance of surplus seating capacity for the (largely mythical) 'big occasion'.

A frequent solution is to create a gathering place by dividing off the westernmost bays of the nave, hopefully incorporating where at all possible the main entrance so that the community can enter the place of liturgical assembly via the gathering place. In this way, welcomes can be made, greetings completed and books given out, before entering the assembly for a period of quiet reflection before worship begins. Anything that we can do through layout and design to help silence the inane chatter of congregations as they (presumably) prepare to meet the Lord of Lords will strike a blow for the Kingdom.

St Paul, Armitage Bridge, Huddersfield.
Richard Shepley

Sometimes dividing a gathering place from a worship area can be achieved by erecting folding screens to allow the narthex to be used as an overflow space on special occasions. Although popular in principle with many congregations (through undue optimism about numbers), the reality can be different. A folding or movable screen can give an unresolved, temporary look to the improvements; and where glazing predominates, they can produce a 'goldfish bowl' feel to the narthex, offer poor sound insulation, and be a more expensive solution than solid screen walls.

In fact, the worshipping communities that shout loudest about lost seats are often those who long ago lost the people to sit in them. Where the church community is genuinely short of worship space, far better to hold a second service, or simply pack everyone in tight for the special occasions (it does wonders for one's image!).

The same area is of course a boon after the eucharist, when the community can socialise and welcome others in comfortable surroundings and stay on for a communal meal if desired.

St Catherine, Sandal
(Ashfield Architects)

In the creation of a gathering place, it is essential to declare war on the 'church hall syndrome' which imprisons our communities in zones of environmental deprivation amidst broken furniture, torn curtains and bare boards, all experienced to full effect beneath the unforgiving glare of fluorescent lights. No wonder we Christians sometimes feel at a disadvantage in this world!

In contrast, our gathering place should boast the best materials, a high degree of comfort, and superb lighting. Unless the community can commit itself to such an approach, it would be better to wait a little longer before attempting such a project. The breweries are the people to watch; they know exactly how (apart from their addiction to games machines!) to spend money wisely to create the right ambience which will encourage people to enter, to linger, to chat and (in their case) to spend money. We have a higher motivation, but should remember our Lord's comment about learning a few tricks from the 'sons of this world' (Luke 16.8).

Reflection: Do we accept the link between hospitality and church growth? Do our existing facilities reflect a high priority for hospitality in our church life?

Group Exercise: Work through the following check list to assess your own situation:

1. If your community has no gathering place, address the issue as a matter, in the first instance, of pastoral strategy, not architecture. What are your community's priorities concerning the space available within your building?

2. If your community already has a gathering place, how can it be improved to be more of a family home and less of a church hall? Where does this come in our community's list of priorities?

3. Do our community's kitchen and gathering space allow us to offer the level of hospitality we consider necessary as an aid to our work of evangelisation and nurture?

4. Does our community's gathering place provide us with a home to which we are proud and delighted to invite our friends?

5. Does our gathering space provide us with sufficient separation between the ministry of welcome and the offering of the liturgy? Do we use the gathering place effectively as a means of preserving an atmosphere of prayerful silence within the area of liturgical assembly?

6. Are there ways in which we could make further use of the gathering place as a means of building up our common life – e.g. by sharing meals together there on some Sundays or Feast Days?

7. What secular buildings in our locality help us understand the importance of creating ambience to further the aims of the organisation concerned?

St Catherine, Wakefield

22

The place of liturgical assembly

St Gregory of Nyssa, San Francisco; outdoor baptistry seen from the eucharistic space

The parish of St Gregory of Nyssa, San Francisco (above), has placed its baptistry in the garden, glimpsed through the windows of the place of eucharistic assembly, for the very good reason that, in today's culture, hospitality precedes commitment, and that therefore the open table should be the first thing encountered by those seeking God in the unconditional love of Jesus of Nazareth.

(1) THE PLACE OF INITIATION

The place of initiation is that area within our building in which baptisms take place and which serves as a permanent reminder to the whole community of the importance of Holy Baptism as our entering into the death and resurrection of Jesus the Christ, and thereby into the holy, priestly community of God.

In the Early Church the place of initiation was in a separate room of the house of the church, and later, when the Church had buildings of its own, the baptistry was often a separate building altogether, thus symbolising the significance of baptism as the first stage on the journey.

Today, opinions among liturgical experts seem to vary as to just how separate the baptistry should be, and this gives the local community a degree of freedom in developing its own particular response to this liturgical need*. What everyone does agree on however, is the necessity for the place of initiation to be more than a font in the corner, but a place of permanent significance clearly demarcated from the rest of the area of liturgical assembly.

Because the place of initiation is not only a place for baptism, but also for the renewal of baptismal vows, for confirmation, for admission to the catechumenate, and for (at least occasionally) the penitential rite at the eucharist, it needs to be in a position which helps us understand our Christian life as journey. It therefore needs to be in an area between the gathering place and the place of eucharistic assembly – possibly in a separate room, or at least in a clearly defined space at the entrance in to the area of assembly.

The baptistry might even be placed in the gathering place itself. This seems a strange notion at first hearing, but a great deal depends on the character of the gathering place or narthex. Provided that the gathering place is large enough to allow the baptistry dignity and space, avoiding any risk that the font will end up looking like a beached whale amid the coffee cups, then there is much to be said for linking the ministry of welcome to the sacrament whereby God welcomes us all into the Church.

If the narthex is used liturgically 'it could be adapted for the celebration of baptism and for an area of welcome, since it is fitting that the welcome and greeting of the members of the community be within the context of the means through which they entered into that community.'

Johnson & Johnson, *Planning for Liturgy*, p. 40

Evry Cathedral; Mario Botta

One thing is certain; the font should never be in the sanctuary. To place a font in the sanctuary, lined up with the ambo and altar on a kind of liturgical stage, deprives it of dignity and reduces it to a mere object among many, instead of the central feature in a distinct area of liturgical activity. Increased visibility for an assembly too lazy to move around is no excuse. Such provision assumes fixed seating and an assembly that is static, spatially if not theologically.

Another certainty is that the font should be a permanent and fixed feature, neither wheeled out from a sacristy nor brushed under the carpet. It is ironic that those communities most anxious to reassert the importance of Baptism by installing a baptismal pool in their building, will often show no interest in expressing it as a permanent architectural feature.

'when we consciously dip our hand into the baptismal water, we embrace this transformation (of Baptism) again and again.'

Regina Kuehn, *A Place for Baptism*, p. 7

Because nothing could be of greater importance in our preparation for worship than our renewed awareness of being the community of the baptised, we need to see the water, touch it and hear it. Water should well up in our assemblies, splashing and gurgling, reminding us constantly of Jesus' promise of a 'spring of water welling up to eternal life' (John 4.14). It should not be mean and mealy-mouthed but joyous and

A dried-up well,
South Yorkshire

St Charles Bornomeo,
Orlando, Florida

Metz Cathedral

extravagant. It is water itself (not its container) which is the primary symbol of baptism, and it should be readily available to every member of the community entering the assembly.

Where there is a fine font cover, hang it high *above* the font; never allow it to remain sitting on the font itself, obscuring the water. The prophet Hosea's 'miscarrying womb and dry breasts' (Hosea 9.14) have nothing on a covered or empty font as a symbol of the abdication of motherhood. The Church is our mother, and the waters of baptism our mother's milk.

When a community comes to design or re-order its place of initiation, the actual details of the structure to contain the water are secondary to the liturgical action which the construction will make possible.

First of all the community must decide which method of baptism – or mixture of methods – will normally prevail in their assembly:
– affusion; when water is poured over the candidate
– immersion; when the candidate is dipped three times into the water
– submersion; when the candidate is completely submerged beneath the surface of the water

From this policy decision – only to be taken after careful study of the history of Christian initiation rather than from seeing a font we take a fancy to in the parish down the road – the design will begin to take shape as we daydream about the practical ways in which the frequent use of water in our liturgies might be used to recall us to our vocation as the community 'baptised by water and the Spirit'.

We are given a whole host of designs in the pattern book of the Early Church – cruciform, hexagonal, octagonal, fonts like graves and fonts like wombs – and a book like Regina Kuehn's *A Place for Baptism* will provide a whole host of useful ideas. What matters is that the community studies these and then 'does its own thing' to bring baptism to life in its own particular setting.

The baptistry also gives us one of the best opportunities to include in the building, with the help of a craftsman stone-cutter or calligrapher, baptismal texts from scripture (anything except Matthew 19.14!) or from the Early Fathers to remind us of our rich heritage. Preferably such texts should be cut into the font itself, as at Portsmouth Cathedral.

Frequently, the font will provide for more than one method of baptism, with different approaches for infants and adults, and this difference in the levels and sizes of pools can be turned to great advantage by incorporating moving water cascading from one pool to another.

Bearing in mind that water is a frightening as well as a refreshing element, life-threatening as well as life-giving, the font should contain sufficient volume of water to speak of both capabilities; it should be big enough to drown in, reminding us that the water of baptism symbolises a death through which we pass into life. We are thus taken once and for all beyond that stage in the Church's stunted growth symbolised by the piece of dried up sponge in the holy water stoup. Indeed, a stoup is superfluous once we have a full and properly sited font.

The place of initiation will therefore have about it a celebratory air, the bubbling waters of the font as welcome as a fountain in an Italian hill village on a baking hot day. The community must accord it a central place in their life together, to ensure that the font is never again reduced to a receptacle for flowers in a dingy corner of the north aisle. If those abandoned fonts represented what Baptism meant to us, no wonder we have had a low opinion of our membership of the Body of Christ.

Here at the waters of new birth, the community recollects, every time it enters the place of assembly, its common baptismal vocation; it seeks, every time it offers the eucharist, the mercy of God; it witnesses,

Ss Peter & Paul Cathedral,
Indianapolis

each Easter, the admission of catechumens to the journey of faith and of the newly baptised to the Body of Christ; it professes its faith and remakes its vows of loyalty to its Master.

Reflection: What importance does baptism hold for our community as an on-going experience? Does the siting and design of our baptistry help us to celebrate and proclaim the centrality of baptism?

Group Exercise: Work through this check list with your own community in mind:

1. Initiate a period of education and reflection in which the community ponders the meaning of its baptismal vocation.

2. From this process, determine what the community would wish to emphasize in the rites of Christian initiation and rededication.

3. How can the Place of Initiation, by its location and its design, best express these insights?

4. How can every member of the community be helped to recall his or her own baptism every time we enter the place of assembly?

5. How can the community be helped to recall its common baptismal vocation when it meets as an assembly?

6. Is the precious gift of water presented in the midst of our assembly in such a way as to proclaim unequivocally and joyously that God-given 'spring of water welling up to eternal life'?

7. How can we regularly enjoy the touch of water in our liturgical assembly? Have we considered the sprinkling of the community from the font as part of the penitential rite, to the accompaniment of an appropriate liturgical song?

St Gregory of Nyssa, San Francisco

23

The place of liturgical assembly

(2) THE PLACE OF THE WORD

The place of the Word is the main liturgical arena of the house of the Church, where the community, having reflected on its baptismal vocation, assembles to encounter the living Lord in the word of God, and to prepare itself for the breaking of the bread and thereafter for its engagement with the world. It is therefore the primary area of liturgical formation, the place where the liturgical assembly spends most of its time, where it is most at home.

The central feature of the Place of the Word is the ambo, the table of the word. In the first Christian basilicas, the ambo was that single piece of liturgical furniture which combined the functions of both lectern and pulpit. In the Early Church the ambo was a considerable structure standing on a raised platform in the middle of the nave facing east, with the community gathered around it.

Ambo at Plymouth Cathedral

If we have inherited a traditional building consisting of nave and chancel, we are given plenty of scope to create a Place of the Word occupying the whole of the nave with an ambo installed in the midst of the assembly. The ambo should face east in order to emphasize the continuing journey of the assembly from the Place of Initiation, through the Place of the Word, on to the Place of the Breaking of the Bread. Furthermore, an eastward facing ambo gets us away once and for all from the suggestion of a line-up of important people doing important things on a 'stage' at the east end, entertaining an 'audience' seated before them.

'For the word of God is living and active, sharper than any two-edged sword, piercing to the division of soul and spirit, of joints and marrow, and discerning the thoughts and intentions of the heart.'

Hebrews 4.12

Just as the Place of Initiation is more than a font, but a place where we are recalled to our vocation and where good liturgical habits are fostered within us, so the Place of the Word is more than an ambo. It is a place where we are chastened and comforted, challenged and exhilarated by the word of God.

Huddersfield

The *General Instruction of the Roman Missal (1969)* states that 'the dignity of the word of God requires' that normally the ambo should be a fixed structure and not just a movable stand (Ch. V. VII). It is helpful if the ambo, like the altar, can look like a table – 'the table of the word' – to represent the equal importance of word and action in the eucharist. If however the ambo and altar are immovable fixtures, the community may find itself severely restricted when it comes to change of layout or experimentation.

This Place therefore becomes for us a shrine of the word, and the community should delight to find ways of expressing reverence for the scriptures in just the same way that Christians have honoured the Blessed Sacrament or the tomb of a martyr. Here we can learn from Jewish practice in the synagogue, in the reverence shown towards the scroll of the Torah as it is carried from the Ark to the lectern; men will reach out to touch the scroll with the edge of their prayer shawls, which they will then put to their lips.

San Francisco

The ambo should be designed not only for reading and preaching the word, but for the display of the open Book of the Gospels (itself embellished with a cover of great beauty and with ribbons), with a lamp constantly burning, and perhaps an icon of Christ Pantocrator and space for individuals to light a candle here. Members of the community should be encouraged to kiss the open book when they enter the place of assembly, or as the book is carried in procession and shown to the assembly at the reading of the Gospel.

Because such expressions of reverence for the word of God have lain dormant for centuries, we need to experiment and to devise ways of such honouring appropriate to our own community, while making a determined effort to overcome our crippling liturgical self-consciousness.

If we would really like to throw caution to the winds, perhaps we should experiment with a single table for both proclaiming the word and breaking the bread. Such a table could be designed to be carried in procession (just like the altar described in Exodus 27) from one liturgical space to another, acting first as ambo and then as altar in the developing eucharistic action. Such an adventurous arrangement would certainly leave our pilgrim status in no doubt.

Because the Place of the Word is where the community will be seated and 'at home' for the greater part of the liturgical action, the seating plan is of the utmost significance.

Just as the 'feel' of a committee meeting will be determined to a large extent by the way we set out the chairs beforehand – round a table, or in a semi-circle, or in rows facing a platform – so the nature of a liturgical assembly will be determined by the seating plan. An assembly sitting in tidy rows facing the same way will expect to be instructed and entertained, whereas an assembly sitting in a semi-circle, or facing one another in choir formation, will expect to participate and to exercise ministry.

Flexible seating is therefore essential if a real process of liturgical formulation is going to be stimulated every time the assembly meets for worship. Not only do we need to break free from centuries of captivity in serried ranks of pews, but we need also to be frequently ringing the changes in our seating plan to denote different 'moods' of the assembly appropriate to different seasons of the Church's Year, and to ensure that we never settle down for too long in any one place, but instead, as God's pilgrim people, are constantly re-pitching the tent. For large parts of the year an anti-phonal arrangement may be appropriate, at other times an arc of seating embracing the ambo, at other times a complete circle. For all these reasons, the removal of fixed pews is a non-negotiable top priority.

Flexibility is the key to a place of liturgical assembly which never dates, for while there is space there is hope. Here, the way in which the two cathedrals in Liverpool play liturgical leapfrog is instructive. The neo-gothic Anglican cathedral was made to look a museum piece by the Roman Catholic Cathedral completed in 1967 with its bold and uncompromising circular seating plan around a central altar. Today however, the Anglican cathedral is seen with fresh eyes, as the full potential of its vast interior and uncluttered spaces is increasingly realised.

Although a platform will award the ambo greater dignity and prominence, there is much to be said for the ambo (as with the altar) standing on the same floor level as the seating, to emphasize the equal accessibility of the whole priestly community to the sacred things of God. This is a teaching symbol of the utmost significance in our rediscovery of our shared vocation. If visibility is likely to be a problem, we should reverse the usual order of things, and install seating on platforms which descend to a central area on which stand the main items of liturgical furniture.

St Anne's Convent,
Melbourne, Kentucky;
Bill Schickel

So far we have been concerned with the attempt to establish a space dedicated to the Word alone, but where we have a single space in which are set the symbols of both word and sacrament, the order in which they are presented may vary. In these situations there is, for example much to be said for setting the ambo at the east end, symbolically 'presiding over' the proceedings, with the sacred meal taking place 'under' the authority of the Word of God. Interestingly,

'The solution is not merely the inclusion of women or married persons into the existing caste of the ordained. It rests rather in the entire community's discovery of its priesthood and in its capacity to take responsible ownership of the rituals'.

Gerard Pottebaum, *The Rites of People*

Film Museum, Dublin

it is Roman Catholic communities in the United States who in this are reviving a layout long revered in the Protestant tradition.

Whatever the sequence in which the liturgical foci are placed within the worship space, ways should be explored of emphasizing the liturgical pilgrim route through the building, by different floor surfaces or even by lighting set within the floor.

All that we have said about the rediscovery of our common vocation as the holy priestly people of God will be further enhanced if the chair of the ordained presider, although remaining distinguishable in some way, is placed alongside the seats of the rest of the assembly (see chapter 26). In this way is the important statement made that the ordained presider emerges *from the assembly* in order to exercise the ministry of leadership and co-ordination; one ministry among many exercised by the community in its shared offering of the liturgy. The leader re-pitches his or her own tent alongside everyone else's.

Reflection: Does our community pay sufficient honour to the word of God in our assembly? In what ways might we give greater prominence to the word?

Group Exercise: Work through the following check list together:

1. Initiate a process by which the community can carefully consider the most appropriate way of creating a Place for the Word.

2. Could the existing nave be cleared of fixed seating and converted in to a place of assembly with a flexible seating plan around a new ambo?

3. Where in your existing building could a new ambo be most effectively placed, and which way should it face?

4. In what ways might members of the community be encouraged to show reverence to the word of God, enthroned permanently at the ambo?

5. In what ways might the assembly, in ritual and gesture, show greater reverence for the Word of God during the liturgy?

6. What seating plan would most accurately express the nature of your community? Where should the seat of the ordained presider be placed for the liturgy of the word?

7. Would it be appropriate for us to experiment with a single table to act as both ambo and altar, carried in procession between the two liturgical spaces involved?

8. Where we have a single space in which both ambo and altar table are set, what order should they take to best express the theological understanding of our own community of faith?

Liverpool Anglican
Cathedral

Blackburn Cathedral

24 The place of liturgical assembly

(3) THE PLACE OF THE BREAKING OF THE BREAD

The Place of the Breaking of the Bread is that area of the house of the Church in which the liturgical assembly gathers to celebrate the ritual meal which recalls those occasions when the Risen Lord made himself known to his followers in the breaking of the bread (recalling his last meal with them before he died), and which looks forward to the heavenly banquet described in the Revelation (Rev. 19.9). At this sacred meal, the priestly community offers gifts of bread and wine, recites a prayer of thanksgiving over the gifts, breaks the bread and then shares the gifts as ritual food 'to proclaim the Lord's death until he comes.' (1 Corinthians 11.26)

'We thank you for counting us worthy to stand in your presence and serve you.'
Third Eucharistic Prayer,
ASB, 1980

It is quite possible of course for this action to take place within the same area as that in which the assembly broke open the word of God, but it is far preferable that it should take place in a further space (which may vary in degree of separation) symbolising the ever onward journey of the people of God. In a traditional building of chancel and nave, the chancel (possibly with side aisles thrown in) might make a very suitable area for this eucharistic action, provided that it is given a completely new look to get us beyond ideas of choir stalls, fenced sanctuaries and altars up flights of steps. Because the assembly stands to offer the eucharistic prayer and to share the bread and the cup, this area should contain no seating apart from a few seats along the walls for the elderly or infirm.

'The Latin word for this part of the church is not sanctuarium but presbyterium. The sanctuary is a sacred place because of the presence of the altar, around which the whole worshipping community is gathered.'

Johnson & Johnson, *Planning for Liturgy*, p. 24

'The cube disappeared . . . so the altar became permanently a sideboard.'

O'Connor, *Why Revive the Liturgy?*, p. 21

'This consecrated table, this altar stands here, Christ in our midst, the center of our life.'

David Philippart, *Saving Signs, Wondrous Words*

St Benoit de Chauveroche, Giromagny

'The people of God, then, are a priestly people, or simply, as the New Testament says, a priesthood.'

J. D. Crichton, *Christian Celebration: the Mass*, p. 36

This area which we traditionally (and most un-helpfully) call the 'sanctuary' is set apart only in so far as it is set apart *for* the altar-table. It must never be thought of as being set apart *from* the people, for it is the people – the whole of the priestly community – who are the sacred ministers gathered around the altar-table to make eucharist.

This begs the question as to what we should call the item of furniture around which the priestly assembly stands to offer the eucharistic prayer. 'Altar' is the word used ever since the Church had buildings of any kind, but it is a little dodgy in New Testament terms as the new altar and sanctuary which Christ by his sacri-fice of himself has made available to us is clearly a heavenly concept not an earthly structure (Heb. 10.19–22). Furthermore, we have seen how as stone replaced timber in these structures, so did a hierarchi-cal and sacerdotal concept of ministry replace the more participatory model of a community sharing a meal around a 'table'.

Nevertheless, priesthood there is in the New Testa-ment: the priesthood of the whole community (1 Peter 2.9) and a priesthood needs an altar as a focus of its work of offering 'spiritual sacrifices acceptable to God through Jesus Christ' (1 Peter 2.5). With the lessons of history staring us in the face however, we cannot but be aware of our capacity to abuse this concept. Wor-shipping communities have been only too happy to offload responsibility onto a professional priesthood, which is in turn only too happy to disappear through a curtain into a holy of holies. In this way have we deprived the whole community of its common voca-tion and taken ourselves back to where we started before the work and teaching of Jesus the Christ. In the end, perhaps only 'altar-table' will do justice to both elements of sacrifice and meal, and to all the richness of our Christian tradition.

'The ideal and indeed ancient form is that of a cube.'

Johnson & Johnson, *Planning for Liturgy*, p. 16

'It must be an altar and not a repository; cubic in shape.'

O'Connor, *Why Revive the Liturgy?*, p. 18

St Charles Borromeo, Orlando, Florida

St Peter, Plymouth

'The Living God's altar has become a dining table'.

David Philippart, *Saving Signs, Wondrous Words*

With all this in mind, the altar-table needs to be a strong simple structure of dignity and beauty of a size which will relate scale to the size of the area or room in which it stands. It should be square in shape (as indeed was the original altar of the Israelites: Ex. 27.1) in order to emphasize that there is no 'back' or 'front' and that it is not a 'counter' across which the assembly is being 'served a meal' by a member of a priestly caste; all members of the priestly community participate in the offering and all have equal access.

To spell out the same point about equal access, the altar should stand on the floor, not on a platform, in the middle of the space. This level approach is a feature of the first altar of Moses (Exodus 20.26), as mentioned in chapter 2.

Choosing the materials for the altar-table will be a valuable exercise for the community of faith in deepening its understanding of what we are about when we offer eucharist. In the wake of Vatican II, the *General Instruction of the Roman Missal (1969)* reveals the tension between the different functions which this one piece of furniture must fulfil. It clearly recognises that the altar 'is also the table of the Lord', but at the same time retains a strong presumption in favour of natural stone 'according to the traditional practice of the Church and the meaning of an altar'. It goes on to say however, that 'any solid, becoming, and skilfully constructed material' may be used with appropriate episcopal approval (*General Instruction of the Roman Missal*, Ch. V. IV).

Whatever materials we use, they should be of the highest quality, and whether built of wood or stone, the end result should look like a table. Given our tendency over the last 2000 years to retreat into sacerdotalism, perhaps we should err on the side of using timber. By this however, we do not mean the flimsy little tables inserted as nave altars in the past. Here we are dealing with the one single altar-table in the liturgical assembly, the focus of its sacramental life, and it must be made to fit both the space and the purpose.

Elmore Abbey, Berkshire.
Norman Davey

'And if you make me an altar of stone, you shall not build it of hewn stones; for if you wield your tool upon it you profane it.'

Exodus 20.25

'At any cost we must rid ourselves of the monstrous accretions before our worship can again be reasonable.'

O'Connor, *Why Revive the Liturgy?*, p. 18

We look in vain to the English Cathedrals to show us how this should be done with sufficient boldness, and it is left to St Giles' Cathedral Edinburgh to show us the way. That the heirs of John Knox should be showing the episcopal churches how to design eucharistic space is a nice touch typical of God's sense of humour.

Whether we use timber or stone, or even some other material, we should make a superhuman effort to restrain ourselves from decorating the altar table. We should let the material and the form speak for themselves, for decoration at this point is quite superfluous. Again, Moses' first altar is a significant model here, for in Exodus 20 Moses is commanded to use rough stones just as they come. God's handiwork has no need of further titivation.

The design of the altar-table should endow it with sufficient strength, beauty and significance to stand in its own right, unadorned with cloths or frontals, candles, cross or flowers.

Provided that the design of the altar table is of sufficient strength and dignity, and its materials of sufficiently fine quality, it should stand completely bare and unadorned when not in use. In this way the altar table stands as a sign of the 'empty stage' of the liturgical arena awaiting the arrival of the people of God, the 'players' in the liturgical drama.

At St Gregory of Nyssa, San Francisco, the altar table greets the visitor on entry, as a sign of the revolution of love in Jesus of Nazareth who ate with publicans and sinners. It also stands in an empty space, allowing the community to stand around it for the eucharistic offering, having *danced* its way there from the place of the word.

'The most ancient adornment of the altar is that which is most likely to go back to the time of Christ himself and the apostles, namely the simple custom of spreading a cloth on the table for a meal.'

Johnson & Johnson, *Planning for Liturgy*, p. 16

The only adornment necessary and appropriate is that of a white linen cloth, laid on the altar-table at the offertory as part of the ceremonies of preparing the table and presenting the gifts.

So that nothing should obstruct the approach to the altar-table, candles should be grouped to one side in standard holders, possibly with the processional cross. All these could be carried in procession, together with banners of the liturgical season, to be placed near ambo or altar-table at different points of the liturgy. Only the sacred vessels containing the gifts should stand on the altar-table during the eucharistic prayer, together with the book.

An altar-table design which would powerfully express the community's nomadic antecedents could of course be one based on that described in Exodus 27. This original altar of the Mosaic covenant was of wood, square in shape and portable, having rings at each corner through which carrying poles could be threaded.

Altar as described in Exodus 27

In today's pilgrim community, such an altar-table could be carried to wherever the liturgical assembly wished to gather – for example out of doors on a suitable festival. As mentioned in the previous chapter, an altar-table of such a design could double up as an ambo which, having served as a table for the breaking open of the word, is carried in joyful procession by the assembly to the place in which it will become the table for the breaking of the bread.

No design could be more resonant with our deepest spiritual origins or more expressive of our calling to be God's people who are constantly on the move, re-pitching our tent.

Seating plan for Maundy
(Holy) Thursday,
St Thomas', Huddersfield

Reflection: Does the siting and design of the altar-table in our community encourage a sense of equal participation in the eucharistic offering? If not, what changes should we be considering?

Group Exercise: Work together through this check list:

1. What word best describes the central feature of the place of the Breaking of the Bread to reflect most accurately the particular story of our community?

2. What word best describes the central feature of the place of the Breaking of the Bread to counteract any historical prejudices which may have coloured our traditional view?

3. What word should we begin to use from now on to do justice to the richness of the Christian tradition?

4. Should our area of the Breaking of the Bread be in the same space as the Place of the Word, or in a separate room or clearly defined space to which the assembly moves as a body?

5. Of what materials should our altar-table be constructed? Should it be so constructed as to be easily portable within the liturgy?

6. Where should we place candles, cross and flowers?

7. How can the movements and gestures surrounding our use of the altar-table help our community to express the themes of pilgrimage and of a shared priesthood?

25

Presiding and praying

(A) THE PLACE OF PRESIDING

Concerning as it does only one person and one chair, the place from which the eucharist is presided over appears at first sight deceptively simple and straight-forward. In fact, the manner in which presidency is expressed is extremely significant in 'giving the game away' as to how a particular community sees itself and its leadership in theological terms.

The Didache – probably the earliest Christian docu-ment outside the New Testament – gives detailed instructions as to how the eucharist is to be offered, and who is to take part, but makes no mention what-soever of who is to preside. Indeed, throughout the Didache it is the whole community that is addressed, suggesting that at that stage the whole community saw itself as celebrant offering together the prayers specified.

Very soon afterwards however, Ignatius of Antioch (martyred AD107) was hammering home the import-ance of the ordained official as the sole guarantor of order and stability, and this internal theological signifi-cance was dressed up in an imperial suit of clothes once Christianity became the official religion of the Empire in AD313. It wasn't long before the chair became the throne.

In subsequent centuries however, the notion of sacri-fice was to dominate eucharistic theology to the exclu-sion of all else. The vision of the priestly community gathered round the altar was lost, and the concept of a presider who, sitting at the east end, 'completed the circle', was lost with it.

'At the Eucharist, offer the eucharistic prayer in this way. Begin with the chalice: "We give thanks to thee, our Father, for the holy Vine of thy servant David, which thou hast made known to us through thy servant Jesus."'

The Didache: Early Christian Writings, p. 231

'Make certain, therefore, that you all observe one common Eucharist; for there is but one Body of Our Lord Jesus Christ, and but one cup of union with His Blood, and one single altar of sacrifice – even as also there is but one bishop, with his clergy and my own fellow-servitors the deacons. This will ensure that all your doings are in full accord with the will of God.'

Ignatius of Antioch, Epistle to the Philadelphians, *Early Christian Writings*, p. 112

St Julie Billiart, Greater Chicago; Guy Prisco

St Augustine, Darlington
(*Fenwick Lawson*)

Presider's *howdah*, St Gregory
of Nyssa, San Francisco

*'The chair of that person
should be clearly in a presiding position, although it
should not suggest either
domination or remoteness.'*

'Environment and Art in
Catholic Worship', para. 70

Liturgical renewal in the wake of Vatican II led to a commendable return to the pattern of the first Christian basilicas in which the chair of the bishop was placed in a presbyterium at the eastern apse behind the altar, with his presbyters seated at either side of him. This arrangement has been re-expressed in the design of contemporary areas of assembly by placing the president's chair at the east end (replacing the high altar as a visual end-stop) with seating for concelebrants in an arc to either side.

In the latest phase of this unfolding story, however, a number of factors are now beginning to mitigate against a slavish adherence to such a layout:

1. The chair in an east end position is often a long way from the seating for the rest of the liturgical assembly, severely detracting from a sense of shared activity. This is especially so in buildings of a traditional gothic plan, where a president seated behind an altar brought forward in the chancel can feel and appear cut off from the main body of the assembly in the nave, and be hampered by poor sight lines. The president can become a remote figure in such a situation, handicapped in calling together the priestly community around the altar of God.

2. Many clergy are uneasy with too patriarchal a style of presiding symbolised by a throne-like chair raised above others' seating levels at the east end. Such unease is in tune with the *General Instruction of the Roman Missal (1969)* which states 'every appearance of a throne should be avoided' (Ch. V. VI).

3. The renewed emphasis on the ordained presider as a member of the priestly community emerging from among the people to exercise his or her particular function, suggests that in due course the president's chair will 'find its natural level' alongside rather than above or beyond. Although this approach can pose problems of visibility and practical convenience, it has much to commend it as a powerful symbol of the shared priesthood of the whole community.

'Chairs or benches for the presiding minister or other ministers, should be so constructed or arranged that they are clearly part of the one assembly.'
'Environment & Art in Catholic worship', para. 70

In the light of these factors, a frequent solution is for the president's chair to be located asymmetrically, possibly in some spatially balanced relationship with the ambo, as at Seattle Cathedral.

Where the liturgical building is conceived of as a single room in which all parts of the eucharistic action take place, the temptation should be resisted to have one place of presiding (nave) for the liturgy of the Word and another (chancel) for the eucharistic meal. The place of presiding should always be located so as to allow the president to co-ordinate the whole of the proceedings from that single position.

Where the renewed emphasis on movement in liturgy gives renewed meaning to the liturgical building as a series of inter-connected rooms or liturgical spaces, then the single and static place of presiding is no longer appropriate. Instead, a place of presiding needs to be established in each liturgical space as the community moves as a body from the place where it has heard and reflected on the word, to the place where, gathered around the altar-table, it will offer the eucharistic prayer and break bread.

On no account should such a concept of liturgical movement be symbolised merely by the president alone moving while the rest of the community remains stationary. In such ways are the roles of both president and community demeaned.

(B) THE PLACE OF PRAYER

Ever since the Church acquired buildings for its exclusive use, the house of the Church has been a place, not only for the corporate prayer of the whole liturgical assembly, but also for the prayer of the individual and of the small group. It is all the more astonishing therefore, to find how few of our liturgical buildings are equipped for this purpose.

The chapel at St Thomas' Huddersfield, converted from an old vestry two years before the re-ordering of the rest of the building.

Except where the existing building is small in scale and intimate in character, provision for private prayer will demand the setting apart of a distinct and separate space. The need for such a space dedicated to prayer alone will be all the more acute in the case of re-ordered buildings with a significant degree of use by the wider community, both because of increased need for an oasis of quiet, and increased opportunity to put before all users the centrality of prayer in the life of the host community.

For all kinds of reasons – theological, liturgical and practical – this separate space for private prayer provides the ideal location for the Reservation of the Blessed Sacrament. At this point however, we come face to face with the deep-seated nostalgia for the days when the tabernacle on the high altar provided both a glorious visual focus for the whole worship space and a triumphalist political statement at the same time. But if we really mean what we say about the Blessed Sacrament being a focus of our devotional prayer rather than an ecclesiological totem, then its location in a place apart, where we can get down to some serious praying, wins every time.

'It is highly recommended that the holy eucharist be reserved in a chapel suitable for private adoration and prayer.'

General Instruction of the Roman Missal, Ch. V. X

Where no separate room or space is available, the Blessed Sacrament should be reserved in such a way that an adequate degree of privacy and quiet is provided round the tabernacle or aumbry, so that individuals can be still and recollected before this supreme sign of the presence of the Lord. This rules out exposed positions of great prominence in the overall space, or through-routes of any kind, or places adjoining busy parts of a church building. A transept for example, might well provide a suitable location, perhaps with lighting and screening (with possibly a canvas canopy above?) to produce a degree of intimacy and enclosure.

Indeed, the creation of such a space will often pre-date the re-ordering of the rest of the building, simply because the process of liturgical formation most commonly begins with a small but committed group praying and reflecting together. The chapel (or whatever such space comes to be called) becomes the spiritual engine-room of the whole community.

The creation of a satisfactory place of prayer is more complex than at first it appears, and requires attention to the following points:

1. Access: the chapel needs to be easily accessed, to encourage spur-of-the-moment use without embarrassment or inconvenience. Preferably it should be near the entrance, avoiding the need to pass through the length of the worship area, and should be clearly marked and have a window in the door to enable visitors to see immediately if it is in use.

Sometimes it is possible to provide a convenient separate access to enable the chapel to continue in use even when the rest of the building is locked.

2. Privacy: the chapel should provide a quiet environment undisturbed by noise from other users of the building.

3. Comfort: the chapel should be separately heated, so that it can be kept warm throughout the winter, even when the rest of the building is not in use. The floor should be carpeted to allow people to kneel or sit without recourse to hassocks.

4. Clear purpose: although the chapel should be warm and comfortable, it is not a lounge or counselling room, and should not look like one. Seating should be around the perimeter, consisting of benches fixed into the walls, not old pews parked against them. The main floor area should remain free of furniture, to give maximum flexibility for different forms of prayer activity.

'Most appropriately, this reservation should be designated in a space designed for individual devotion . . . (in a) room or chapel specifically designed and separate from the major space.'
Environment & Art in Catholic Worship para. 78

5. Beauty: a visual focus for devotion should be provided, such as an icon, sculpture or other artwork (see

Appendix B). The lighting of candles is a custom growing in popularity irrespective of Christian tradition, and should be catered for in the chapel, giving due regard to the fire risk by adequate supervision.

6. Lighting: because the chapel will be used primarily for private prayer, lighting should be soft, with fittings fixed low down in the space, perhaps lamps standing on the floor. Narrow-beamed spotlights should pinpoint the visual or liturgical foci and directional lighting should also be included above the bench seating to enable the Office of Morning and Evening Prayer to be said corporately by small groups.

7. Exclusive use: the chapel should be used for no other purpose than prayer, no matter how great the pressure on space pertaining in the rest of the building. The setting apart of this space for prayer will imbue the room with a distinctive character which would be immediately undermined by any form of dual use. If this requires a sacrificial gift of valuable space to the activity of prayer, it will say more about the Church's priorities than a season of sermons.

8. Reservation of the Blessed Sacrament: such a chapel would provide the most appropriate location for Reservation, as it removes any possible confusion between the celebration of the eucharist (at the altar-table) and its reservation (in a place set apart) for communion of the sick and as a focus for private prayer.

9. Altar-table: because there should only be one altar-table in the house of the Church, it is preferable that the chapel should contain no altar-table. The eucharist for groups smaller than the main liturgical assembly should be celebrated in the main place of assembly, possibly by using the altar-table in a different position, or facing in another direction. In circumstances where the main area of assembly does not provide a convenient or helpful setting for a weekday eucharist (this may depend on the time of the year), an altar-table

might have to be placed in the chapel, but this should not be a permanent fixture.

Reflection:

(a) Presiding –

1. Where is the most effective place for the president's chair, to enable the presider to see and be seen, and to express most clearly the kind of community we are?

2. How can the president's chair be given simple dignity and distinctiveness while avoiding separation and remoteness?

(b) Praying –

1. How can our community encourage greater use of our building for private prayer?

2. If Reservation of the Blessed Sacrament is our tradition, should the place of reservation be moved into the chapel?

3. If Reservation is not our tradition, should we consider making it so?

Exercise:
1. Walk round your building, examine the provision for private prayer and discuss how far it would meet the needs of a stranger seeking out a place of quiet in your building.

2. If the community's building does not yet contain a place of private prayer, where would a chapel be most appropriately located?

3. If your building already contains a place of private prayer, examine its adequacy in the light of the nine points set out above, and draw up a programme of improvements.

Making music

'Therefore sacred music will be the more holy the more closely it is joined to the liturgical rite, whether by adding delight to pray, fostering oneness of spirit, or investing the rites with greater solemnity'.

Constitution on the Sacred Liturgy (1963), VI. 112

The process by which the focus of priesthood is shifting from the specialist to the whole community is now being echoed in the making of music in the liturgical assembly.

In more and more parish communities, music is being rediscovered as an activity no longer the preserve of an elite group who dress differently and sit in special seats, but a possession of the whole assembly responding to the call to the whole people of God to 'be filled with the Spirit, addressing one another in psalms and hymns and spiritual songs, singing and making melody to the Lord with all your heart'. (Ephesians 5.19)

The Constitution on the Sacred Liturgy (1963) rightly recognises the musical tradition of the Church as pre-eminent among the arts relating to liturgy in that 'as a combination of sacred music and words, it forms a necessary or integral part of the solemn liturgy'. (*Constitution on the Sacred Liturgy*, VI. 112). This rings true whatever our tradition, for music is not bolted on to the liturgy as an optional extra but is part and parcel of the whole offering of worship.

No one should ever doubt the power of music to make or break good liturgy. It can be a source of inspiration and spiritual unity second to none, or it can divide and

polarize faith communities, and reduce musicians and singers to performers in a concert rather than participants in a sacred rite. It is essential that we get it right if we are to renew our liturgies, and an important aspect of getting it right is to move away from professionalisation and elitism to restore music to the whole assembly.

In England, the nineteenth-century legacy of the robed choir greatly hampers us in this task. This comparatively recent invention illustrates how the Victorians' flight into medieval romance swamped all other considerations. Inserting choir stalls into our local neighbourhood chancel was in essence a popish idea, harking back to Gregory the Great and Palestrina, but was taken up with equal gusto by 'Low' and 'High' alike, such was the craving for all things gothic.

Irrespective of churchmanship, the Victorian Church's approach to the making of music in worship was basically regressive, taking us back to the 'good old days' of religion. Out went the parish band familiar to us from Hardy's novels – a rather motley crew of rude peasants bowing and scraping up in the west gallery – and in came the surpliced choir of gentlemen, dressed up like clerics, enthroned in a specially reordered chancel with 'monastic' choir stalls set behind a chancel screen, and with an organ – a proper gothic (i.e. Christian) instrument – to accompany them.

In this way was the nineteenth century Church dragged screaming back into the Middle Ages when making music in the liturgy was restricted to the professionals, while the *hoi polloi* were reduced to the role of spectators. Thus the English Church of the nineteenth century aped the Italian Church of the seventeenth, with its professional musicians hijacking the people's liturgy and turning it into an exclusive, union-controlled operatic performance.

'Before 1860, few of our parish churches had organs. People sang to a church band – there is something to retort to those who accuse your music group of trendiness!'

Robert Maguire
Liturgy North 96

'What in reality so often happens in many churches is that the music divides the musicians from the congregation . . . this geographical separation of the forces is a hazard, made the more so because it is all contrary to the togetherness and involvement which is at the heart of contemporary liturgical thinking.'

Lionel Dakers, *RSCM Quarterly*, January 1988

'For the congregation, watching from a distance was considered sufficient. Music developed as a professional enterprise that took on a life of its own apart from the worship''.

Edward Foley, *From Age to Age*, p. 103

Yes of course the Victorians did make some concessions in that they allowed us all to sing hymns, but hymn singing can be a fairly exclusive and professional affair whenever the selection of tunes, sources and tempo remain in the hands of a choir more aware of its privileges than its responsibilities, and all too conscious of its solemn duty to protect others from musical bad taste.

All this can leave the contemporary Church with a serious conflict of interests when it comes to re-ordering a building to express a contemporary understanding of the liturgical assembly. The continued existence of a robed choir poses two particular problems:

1. Liturgically, the robed choir, by reason of its historical development, will usually be found occupying a crucial space at the very axis of the building, precisely at the point where the community requires freedom of movement to evolve into the most appropriate configuration for the assembly. Robed choirs are territorially possessive to a high degree.

2. Spatially, the robed choir requires a room set apart for robing and possibly for practising, and this can prove an expensive luxury where there is pressure from a variety of uses converging on limited space.

a homeless choir . . .

In addition the robed choir seems to possess the power to 'haunt' a community long after its demise. Empty choir stalls are polished as religiously as ever, and the blue gowns hanging in the choir vestry have the moths shaken from them regularly, awaiting the day when the jabot shall return. Meanwhile, these sacred sites are seen as shrines to the happier, more glorious days of yesteryear.

Perhaps the following principles may help a community resolve such conflict:

(a) Music is one of the most important ingredients in good worship, widely attested to in the contemporary

Church as a primary factor in the renewal of a community's liturgical life.

(b) The 'choir' should be understood as consisting of the whole assembly, expressing in song its praise and thanksgiving to God.

(c) Within the community, particular individuals and groups will have special musical gifts enabling them to assist the whole assembly in giving voice to its desire to praise God in song.

(d) The musicians concerned should see themselves as part of the assembly, emerging from it during the liturgy as and when required, and then returning to their places. For this reason, distinctive robes, or special liturgical seating, is inappropriate.

Lutheran church, Tübingen

(e) Organists, instrumentalists and singers all have a part to play in enriching the liturgy, and should place themselves at the disposal of the assembly under the direction of a musical co-ordinator who will call upon them as and when required. There is no room for any rivalry between ancient and modern, or between 'choir' and 'music group'; all should form part of the one offering of praise.

(f) Because the Christian community is a single body made up of young and old, progressive and traditional, our liturgy should embrace as many musical traditions as possible, so that we may learn from one another every time the assembly meets to worship. Under no circumstances should the community submit to dividing itself on the basis of a polarisation of musical tradition, formalised in mutually exclusive meetings of the assembly.

(g) Wherever possible the pipe organ should be located at the west end where, removed from the confines of a transept or side chapel, it can 'speak' powerfully and effectively to the whole building, especially if raised on a gallery or platform. Where no gallery exists, its construction can often be combined with that of a western narthex or entrance lobby, above which the organ can be placed, thereby killing two liturgical birds with one stone.

These basic principles have long been familiar to us in the monastic tradition, where the whole community is the choir meeting at various points throughout the day to sing the Office. The tone deaf evidently learn to sing *sotto voce*, while those with special gifts emerge occasionally from their stalls to sing an alleluia or play an instrumental interlude, and then return to their places. No member of the community is dressed differently from anyone else, and no special seats are reserved. The assembly has become the choir.

When it comes to liturgical re-ordering therefore, a much greater flexibility now prevails. In buildings with a pipe organ (especially one with a fixed console) the organist and musicians will need to be able to coordinate their efforts, but otherwise the musicians can usually place themselves in any convenient spot from which the music co-ordinator can be seen by the whole assembly, and from where any necessary plugging in can be done with a minimal amount of trailing wires. But beware – new music group can be old choir writ large when it comes to territorial possessiveness!

Because the assembly celebrates the liturgy using different seating configurations from time to time, the musicians may well find themselves occupying different locations in support of them. Human nature being what it is however, the musicians will no doubt tend to adopt a corner of the area of assembly and make it their own, and this is on the whole sensible provided that they don't fall into the trap of their surpliced forebears and become transmogrified into a sacred immovable object. Not even musicians can be excused tent-pitching duties.

Reflection: Is making music in our community a preserve of the few or a celebration of the whole assembly?

> 'The effect of the organ is very good . . . its position in the west gallery an ideal one. From a liturgical point of view there is not the slightest difficulty, and surely it is preferable that the pipes should have a proper chance of speaking rather than that they should be "cribbed, cabined and confined" in a small chamber.'
>
> G. H. Smith quoted by Richard Hird, *Organists Review*, February 1966

Establishing priorities . . . (car park, Chester Diocese).

Group Exercise: Work through together the following check list;

1. Is the whole liturgical assembly the 'choir' of your community? Have we experienced the liberation of the whole assembly learning to sing in parts, unaccompanied?*

If you doubt this can be done, contact the Iona Community, whose Wild Goose Resource Group has a special gift of creating celestial choirs out of the most unpromising raw material and causing great fun in the process. Address: 840 Govan Road, Glasgow G51 3UU. Tel: 0141 445 4561.

2. How often does it meet to practise its music?

3. Is the community using all the gifts within its membership to help its musical expression and enrich its worship? Do you enjoy a variety of musical accompaniment at every service?

4. Is your community's liturgical life enriched by a variety of musical traditions, or do you connive at hiving off different traditions into separate services for like-minded people?

5. Who or what are the obstacles to change within our community? How can we set in motion the dialogue necessary to bring about change? Are we as a community willing to face the upheaval and conflict which may result?

6. Have we asked for outside specialist help? Is there a locally-based musician – perhaps a member of our diocesan liturgical committee, or Joint Advisory Group or of the Iona Community – who could be invited to give us a training day on some of the new material (and options for accompanying it) now available?

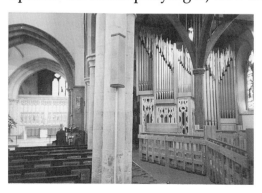

The tail wagging the liturgical dog . . . Great Berkhamsted, Herts

St Michael and All Angels, Sunnyside, Herts

27 Nurture and neighbour

1. Christian Nurture

The blessing given to this generation of Christians is that God has rescued us from going *to* church and shown us what it means to *be* Church.

Integral to this fresh understanding of our calling as followers of Jesus is the realisation that evangelisation is not a matter of handing over a package labelled 'The Gospel', but of embracing others in a way of life, of incorporating them into a living community. Conversion is process rather than event, and it never ends; as Christians, we carry a large 'L' plate on our backs until the day we die.

This truth has repercussions for our community when we come to re-order our building, for we come to realise that even worship and fellowship are not enough. In addition we need to be nurtured in our faith. This applies to all Christians, for at no time in our lives can we afford to sit back and take a rest from our seeking after God, but it applies especially to those who are new and unsure and vulnerable. The Sunday assembly, especially in a growing community, can be a daunting and impersonal experience for the newcomer, and there is need always for a structure of smaller groupings in which the individual can feel more quickly a sense of belonging and of value.

Bacon, scrambled eggs and hash browns.
Parish breakfast, St Anne, West Chester, Ohio

Our buildings need to make provision for these requirements of continuing nurture, for although the private home will continue to provide the most helpful setting for many groups, at other times a central, more neutral venue will be essential. Furthermore, the growing trend towards all-age instruction at the time of the main Sunday assembly demands spaces for a number of groups to meet simultaneously within the building.

Over and above the catering facilities mentioned in chapter 22, which will enable our community to offer the appropriate 'background music' of warm hospitality, the community will need spaces exclusively set aside for nurture.

Basically this accommodation needs to consist of a series of small rooms suitable for learning in groups of various sizes. This does not mean one large room subdivided by folding screens, a solution which always ends up looking not only tatty, but also unworkable.

Holy Trinity, Huddersfield: Children's room on first floor

The kind of accommodation required is often suitable for insertion at first floor level, for example in projects where the west end of an existing building is re-ordered on two levels for a variety of communal activities. Although access for the disabled is to be incorporated wherever possible, it is not usually quite as important for specialist uses of this kind as for public areas on the ground floor.

These rooms should be set aside for small group work, for the catechumenate, and for other work with young people. The community should do a great deal of forward planning in allocating spaces in the field of nurture, aiming to be as realistic as possible in projecting likely demand. Where possible, different groups (e.g. the catechumenate) should be allowed to make one of the rooms their own, and in order to preserve the special character of these spaces, dual use should be restricted to a minimum. The gradual transformation of these rooms into repositories for the community's junk must be resisted!

View from worship area, Holy Trinity, Huddersfield; installation of facilities for Christian nurture on three floors. Peter Wright

People coming into contact with the Church will be accustomed to good facilities in other walks of life, even in times of economic stringency, and the community's teaching rooms must be comfortable and equipped to a high standard to make clear that the Church is not a second rate organisation but one which invests boldly in its future.

Above all, good facilities for nurture will mean the church building hums with life in the evenings as well as throughout the day. This is an important consideration as we strive to give back to the house of the church its rightful role at the centre of the local community.

2. 'And who is my neighbour?'

The lawyer who first asked this question (Luke 10.29) asked it to dodge the demands of the new teaching of Jesus; we need to ask it in a mood of honest humble enquiry, in order to respond gladly to those demands.

A re-ordering project will inevitably provide our community with spaces – e.g. the Gathering Place – which will be underused during the week, especially during working hours. We need to ask ourselves some hard questions as a community about the usefulness of our facilities as a means of making a difference to the lives of any around us who may find themselves in difficulty. Is there any way we can use them to benefit those of our neighbours less fortunate than ourselves? Amongst those in need, which particular group do we feel drawn to, or which group troubles our conscience the most?

Once we have determined who our neighbour is (and we recall that in Jesus' story it was the least likely candidate), we can begin to incorporate into our thinking and planning the architectural repercussions of our decision.

There is every reason to go through this process at the very earliest stage, as Christian communities reordering their buildings will find that potential funding from charitable trusts will depend entirely on the community work component. Churches become eligible for grant aid in so far as the projects proposed will better equip them to serve those in need in their neighbourhood.

Furthermore, grant-making bodies will look for evidence of partnership agreements with other churches and caring agencies, and this must consist not merely of pious hopes, but of well-researched proposals with well-documented support from potential partners and client-groups.

'We need a radically thought-out church building which seeks to call both the gathered Christian community within its walls and the non-christian community outside to a new awareness of God's love.'
Peter Cavanagh, *Church Buildings*, p. 5

The availability of such funding helps concentrate the mind of the Christian community by requiring us to respond positively to Jesus' frightening definition of what it means to be a neighbour.

The community will need to do its homework:

(a) Consult the local authority's social services department and your social responsibility officer (if your diocese has one), to assess prime areas of need in the locality.

(b) Having identified an area of need, discuss with the local authority or with other agencies working in the same field, the possibility of joint action. Even where capital funding is not available, other agencies may well be keen to make use of Church premises on a long-term basis, or to provide supervisory staff during an interim period. It will be necessary to obtain in writing a clear commitment from the agency concerned to use the premises as and when adapted and refurbished.

(c) Feed into the design process the requirements of the user. These will usually be quite specific (e.g. in relation to public health requirements for food preparation, and for disabled toilets) and failure to adhere to them would jeopardise any grant assistance available from the local authority.

(d) Make application to relevant charitable trusts for capital grants towards the costs of adapting your building to cater for those in need. Applications will need to show in detail your thorough groundwork completed under the headings a to c above.

Reflection: Is our community's building a place where people can both learn about the Christian faith and see it in action responding to need? If not, how can we make it so?

Group Exercise: Work through together the following check list:

(a) Nurture –
1. What are your community's existing needs in the field of Christian nurture?

2. In what way might strategic decisions about training and nurture affect future demands for space over the next five years?

3. What priority does your community give to investment in future growth?

4. If your existing building cannot accommodate your training needs, has consideration been given to hiring other premises, e.g. a local school?

(b) Neighbour –
1. Is there any clue, in the recent history of our local community, as to the identity of the 'neighbour' most in need?

2. What particular gifts and skills does our worshipping community possess which may help us identify the area of work in which we may be most effective?

3. Is there any particular glaring social need which troubles us?

4. What existing contacts do we have with the local authority, health authority or other caring agencies in

our area? How can we initiate a process of consultation with them?

5. What charitable trusts or other funding bodies are we aware of with a particular interest in this field of work? How can we find out about others?

Conclusion

If we have followed this handbook through all its stages, reassessing as we go the character and quality of the liturgical expression of our life together as the community of Jesus, the Christ, what do we have?

'Some of the best places are not made so much as remade, as people find new and unforeseen ways to inhabit them over time'.

Pollan, *A Place of my Own*

Certainly we do not have the perfect church building, no more than we can ever have the perfect church community, for there is no blue-print for 'success' hidden in this book or any other. All we have is a set of questions which jolt us out of complacency and conservatism into setting out all over again on the adventure of the open road with God, seeking out the best camping site to pitch our community's tent.

Whenever I have driven to a re-ordering consultation, and have parked outside the building concerned, I always die a little death as I bestir myself to leave the warmth and comfort of the car and enter unknown territory; new faces, new names, perhaps a tricky encounter or an audience that has no wish to listen. I know equally well that, once out of the car and into the thick of things, I shall realise all over again that, at that moment, there is no other place I would rather be.

A local Christian community can become car-bound too; strapped into a warm cocoon, knowing that in due course it must get out and get on, but unwilling to do it right now, forgetting the joy that lies ahead if only (the Americans say it so well) we will 'haul ass'.

If this handbook has helped one or two communities to open the door and begin to move into the unknown, to feel exhilarated by the encounter with others through the energising power of God's Spirit, and to design new spaces for that encounter which honour God and delight one another, then it will have served its purpose.

Liturgy 'is a steady light,
constantly burning;
a gentle flame, continually
warming;
a force, silently at work,
moulding and purifying.'

Romano Guardini, 'Some
Dangers of the Liturgical
Revival', *Unto the Altar*, p. 15

Romano Guardini, the prophetic liturgist and theologian of Germany in the 1930s, described liturgy as 'an irreplaceable pastoral tool'; 'a force, silently at work, moulding and purifying'.

For too long in the English scene we have failed to recognise the vital part that liturgy has to play in shaping our Christian lives, either consigning it to the academic seminar or restricting it to a 'quick fix' on a special occasion when we seek a few extra tingles down the spine. In so doing, we have ignored the 'irreplaceable pastoral tool' of what should rightly be called 'pastoral liturgy' i.e. a liturgy which involves architecture, form, light, space, art and movement as much as rite and rubric, and which embraces us in an overwhelming experience of God's activity and love.

'In simple prayer and
genuine worship even
modern men and women
can find certain values at
a wholly different depth of
their existence, and can
truly experience where we
come from, where we are,
and where we are going.'

Hans Küng, *Why I am still a
Christian*, p. 24

More particularly, because it is above all a communal experience, pastoral liturgy calls us out of self, out of our own little concerns, likes and dislikes, towards our unity with God and with one another in Jesus, the Christ. It gives us a fresh awareness that whenever we assemble as the community of the Baptised, to break open the word of God and to participate in the breaking of the bread, we remember who we are, where we have come from, and where we are going as God's own people.

This handbook will have served some purpose if it has opened our eyes to the opportunities before us as the liturgical assembly to proclaim the wonderful works of God, to delight in being his Spirit-filled people, and to entrust ourselves to the adventure of living out the reckless generous love of God revealed in Jesus.

It will also have served some purpose if it makes us impatient to see the environment of worship transformed to reflect accurately our spirituality and theology, so that in liturgy what we do and say matches what we believe. As yet, this is not the case in most parish churches, and we live out a liturgical half-truth as, fearful of the future, we cling to familiar furniture and tired tunes. For the most part we are content to continue going to church as a means of avoiding becoming the Church.

For better or for worse, the renewal of pastoral liturgy necessary to bring about that transition from church to Church cannot be achieved without a ruthless reassessment of every detail of our buildings' interiors, and the longer we leave it, the worse the pain and upheaval will be. Unavoidably, the crowbar represents a vital stage in our spiritual growth as missionary congregations.

Pastoral liturgy is not an optional extra for those sensitive souls who enjoy artistic things, a minority interest peripheral to the Church as a whole. A church building which, by its enshrining of old idols, mocks week after week the words, hopes and aspirations of the community gathering within its walls, is a scandalous stumbling block for those who come to us saying 'we would see Jesus'.

At the same time pastoral liturgy – no more than any other aspect of spiritual renewal – is not the whole story. The heart of the matter is a living relationship with God experienced afresh in Jesus, and unless our own hearts are in the right place with God we shall toil at re-ordering to no avail, producing merely aesthetic masterpieces which will drug us to sleep with their beauty and reduce us to the state of liturgical lotus eaters.

'It is about working through the building. It is not about designing stylistically interesting furnishings, whether "modern" or, as they say, "period". It is about letting the building itself come alive.'

Robert Maguire,
Liturgy North 96

Given that proviso, it is evident that faithful communities which wait upon the Lord, which pray, and discuss and explore and dream dreams, have been able to transform their tired old buildings into places of assembly which by their beauty, simplicity and meaning heighten consciousness of God's resplendent love, and help shape the living church which they house.

This renewal of our buildings to create sacred spaces which can speak of our renewed vision of God today is nothing less than a conversion experience, not only for others, but for ourselves. In rediscovering our communal need to re-pitch the tent in order to journey into God, we discover our true identity as his pilgrim people.

Once upon a time we set out to go to church, and now find ourselves to be the church. Thanks be to God.

'Not in the dark of buildings confining,
not in some heaven light years away,
but here in this place, the new light is shining,
now is the Kingdom, now is the day.
Gather us in and hold us for ever,
gather us in, and make us your own;
gather us in, all peoples together,
fire of love in our flesh and our bone.'

Mary Haugen (*Celebration Hymnal*, 752)

Appendices

Appendix A: Stages of consultation for re-ordering

Appendix B: Art as an aid to worship

Appendix C: Landscaping

Appendix D: Appointing an architect or consultant in liturgical space

Appendix E: Developing an operational plan

Appendix F: Fundraising

Appendix G: Installation of new lighting schemes

Appendix H: Floor surfaces

Appendix I: 'The Heritage Trail' – some conservation issues

Appendix J: A six-week crash course on the design of liturgical space

Postscript: 'The Magical Mystery Tour'

Appendix A

STAGES OF CONSULTATION FOR RE-ORDERING

(a) The church council (PCC or equivalent body in other traditions) engages in a training day(s) for its own membership which examines the process of liturgical formation, assesses the need in terms of this particular community, and agrees to examine the possibilities in more detail.

(b) The church council sets up a small working party (of around 5 members) to formulate basic ideas for change in the community's built environment, in the light of the experience of other parishes or churches in their area, and as part of a strategy for growth and development. The working group will be given clear terms of reference and a timetable.

(c) In the light of the working group's report, and after further reflection, the church council endorses the process by passing a resolution initiating a comprehensive review of their 'house of the church' in the context of the SDP, and encouraging all members of the community to take part in the process as and when invited to do so. At this stage the whole assembly could be informed at Sunday worship of the direction in which things are moving.

(d) The church council decides what professional help is required, and makes an appropriate appointment. Two or three English dioceses* have already appointed a specialist in this field, equipped to approach re-ordering from a theological perspective, and if so he or she should be consulted at this stage. Alternatively it may be that the Diocesan Advisory Committee (or

* Wakefield, Blackburn and the episcopal area of Stepney

better still the Joint Advisory Group if your diocese is enlightened enough to have one) has someone who can advise as to basic principles and at the design stage. In the United States this role is increasingly fulfilled by a 'consultant in liturgical space', a profession as yet in its infancy in this country. If an architect is required, he or she should be chosen with the utmost care (see Appendix B).

(e) The church council requests its liturgical consultant or architect to assess the existing building in terms of the community's Mission Statement and in close consultation with the council's working group, and to present to the council preliminary proposals as a basis for wider consultation.

(f) Using the preliminary proposals as a basis for discussion, the church council sets in motion a training programme involving the whole worshipping community. Such a programme may last weeks, months, or a whole winter, and will be aimed at going beyond questions of detail to the underlying motives of liturgical formation and mission inherent in the SDP.

(g) The church council informs the appropriate diocesan body of its intentions, and requests comments on its preliminary proposals.

(h) The liturgical consultant or architect is requested to present a detailed scheme to the church council for approval.

(i) The approved proposals are presented to an open meeting for the whole community. Where there is likely to be a great deal of public interest (e.g. in the case of an historic building) it may be advisable to have a presentation to the worshipping community (if possible at Sunday worship) before presentation to a wider public meeting.

(j) In the Church of England, a faculty petition is submitted to the DAC and, where the external appearance of the building is affected, a planning application to the local authority.

'When asked by a DAC to consider 'compromising a situation based on the concern for avoiding change . . . the parish should address the Advisory Committee, through its Chairman, directly on the question of whether his committee is a committee of the Christian Church or an outpost of the Conservation Movement.'

Robert Maguire,
Liturgy North 96

Appendix B

Temporary art: children's Easter banner

ART AS AN AID TO WORSHIP

The following should be borne in mind when considering the place of art in liturgical space:

(a) Decide the main thrust which best expresses the community's insight – empty cross? the Crucified One? Christ in Majesty?

(b) Decide what subsidiary symbols would be helpful – perhaps some representation of Mary or the patron saint of the parish, or symbols from previous generations, e.g. the fish or ichthus sign, or the chi-ro.

(c) If you have a building already containing rich symbolism, decide how this can be reduced to avoid duplication (there should only be one cross and one representation of any saint) and thereby increase the impact of what remains. Minimalism really works!

(d) Make decisions on the basis of what best expresses the life and work of this community now, not on the basis of past allegiance to party churchmanship or of who donated what and when.

(e) For all new work (and in a building already full of symbols, all may need to be replaced with one or two symbols of beauty and power) go to a local artist rather than the catalogue. Surprisingly it need not be any more expensive to commission a unique work of art than to purchase something mass-produced. If you find established names too expensive, proceed to your local college of art or technical college and get the appropriate member of staff to point you in the direction of the rising star. For Anglicans, the Diocesan Advisory Committee is on hand to advise.

Church of the Nativity,
Rancho de Sante Fe,
San Diego

'Ultimately any artwork will inevitably reflect the inner depth of the artist. If he has no depth, no spirituality, this will be evident in his work. The artist needs to experience the spiritual journey for himself if he is to embody this with any authenticity and communicate it to others. If his work is to lead to an authentic journey of prayer, he will need to have undertaken that journey himself.'

Michael Jones Frank,
'Liturgical Art and the Artist',
Church Building Issue 31

(f) Consult your Diocesan Advisory Committee or the Council for the Care of Churches (or equivalent bodies) before commissioning any new work. Cautionary tales abound of irate artists, tearful donors and embarrassed clergy who failed to consult early enough.

(g) Banners can help, but beware of overcrowding, and of home-made banners which no-one likes to be the first to admit to finding atrocious.

Sometimes colour alone (related to the seasons of the Church's year) and the form of the banners, pennants or hangings can speak more powerfully than texts which become hackneyed after we've read them for the 50th Sunday in succession.

(h) Learning from the errors of previous generations, determine never *ever* to allow a dedication plaque anywhere near a donation of a work of art. A list of donors can be kept in a book in the gathering place.

Useful addresses:
Council for the Care of Churches
Fielden House, Little College Street,
London SW1P 3SH. (Tel: 0171 222 3793)

Art and Christianity Enquiry (ACE)
4 Regents Park Road, London NW1 7TX.
(Tel: 0171 485 3077)

Art in Churches
18 Markham Square, London SW3 4UY.
(Tel: 0171 589 0037)

Catholic Bishops' Conference
39 Eccleston Square, London SW1V 1PL.
(Tel: 0171 821 0553)

Christian Arts
40 Thistlethwaite Road, London E5 0QQ.
(Tel: 0181 985 8568)

Appendix C

LANDSCAPING

(a) Some points to remember in landscaping the grounds of church buildings:

1. At the present time, landscaping (like church lighting) is in a parlous state generally; many of the 'experts' just cannot be trusted. Consider for a moment those churchyards which have delighted you most in your life. The chances are that they will be full of mature trees, and the chances are that they will be species of trees unheard of at the local garden centre.

Local garden centres seem to stock only species which pander to suburban man's innate fear of and prejudice against trees, and even local authority landscape departments seem only to have heard of whitebeam, rowan or silver birch – anything which won't annoy the highway engineers.

2. Proceed to the nearest country church with ancient trees and do as our ancestors did. Their planting contributed to the environment of the whole village, not just to that of the churchyard, and ours should do likewise. To help you, seek out the specialist nurseries who deal with the forestry industry. Follow your hunch, and think big.

As an acid test of whether it really believes it has a future, every community of faith should plant a yew tree for the benefit of those who will follow them in about 1000 years time.

3. As a guide in the choice of species –
IN: lime, beech, chestnut, oak, ash, yew, plane,

sycamore (yes, sycamore, the most Scriptural and the most maligned of all our great trees, tough as old boots).
OUT: cherry, willow, silver birch, rowan, whitebeam, alder, any ornamental tree, cypress in any shape or form, rosebeds and other such fussy detail.

4. Where boundaries require defining, outlaw cupressus of any sort, and put in hawthorn (impenetrable if planted closely enough) or beech, behind a temporary fence.

5. In rural areas let the churchyard be as natural as possible; there's nothing more delightful than the contrast between immaculate close-cropped verges and areas of long grass with cow parsley and wild flowers.

6. In urban areas where the building sits hard by the road side, architectural advice should be sought on how best to integrate it with the street. Where space around a building is restricted, boundary walls which serve no purpose other than to hem in litter should be removed and the space behind landscaped with cobbles or other hard surfaces to bring it into the street possibly as a public seating area. The Local Authority may well assist in such a scheme.

7. Where pedestrian desire lines cross the site, accept defeat and make a virtue of them by encouraging well-designed pedestrian access with good lighting which will make the area a safer place and discourage crime.

8. Remember that existing tree cover requires a continual programme of gradual replacement; don't leave it until you have had to fell diseased trees and thereby inflict on the neighbourhood a bare churchyard for a generation.

9. Churchyards and grounds; most dioceses have guidelines for the care of churchyards, and these need to be studied carefully.

Consult your Local Authority with a view to a joint environmental project of benefit to the wider community especially where public safety is a factor for consideration.

If you seek help with manpower for planting or clearing, consult your local volunteer bureau, and local colleges and schools.

In England, if you would like to go for the 'wild look', to create a habitat for wild flora and fauna, you can obtain from the Council for the Care of Churches their booklet *Wild Life in Church and Churchyard*, or consult the Living Churchyard and Cemetery Project, which provides a useful series of information packs and leaflets. The Project can be contacted at the National Agricultural Centre, Stoneleigh Park, Warwickshire, CV8 2LZ.

Monastere St Andre de Clerlande, Belgium

Appendix D

APPOINTING AN ARCHITECT OR CONSULTANT IN LITURGICAL SPACE

In nearly every case of re-ordering an existing building, the local Christian community will require the advice and assistance of a suitably qualified and experienced professional.

In all cases involving structural alterations to an existing building, the help of a qualified architect will be necessary. In cases involving the design of liturgical space, either an architect or a consultant in liturgical space will be the appropriate source of advice and oversight.

Points to watch:
1. Not all architects have experience of the design of liturgical space or awareness of the theological principles involved, and a particular expertise in building conservation does not necessarily mean that an architect is skilled as a designer of new work. A Parochial Church Council or equivalent body contemplating a re-ordering scheme should not therefore feel obliged to engage the services of an architect already working with them as their inspecting architect.

2. When contemplating a re-ordering project, the church council needs first to consider what professional advice is needed and at what stage. For example a consultant in liturgical space, familiar with the theological issues involved, may be required for the early stages of consultation and reflection, helping the community to draw up a detailed architectural brief which can then be handed over to an architect. Alternatively an architect may be engaged to design and construct

'One has to see that keeping old stones sitting on top of one another, and curing outbreaks of dry rot, is a very different, if noble, art than making a church more suitable for modern worship.'

Robert Maguire,
Liturgy North 96

the architectural shell which will then be fitted out as a liturgical space by a liturgical consultant.

3. A church council should never take the easy way out of appointing without proper consideration an architect or consultant they just happen to know. At least three candidates for any appointment should be interviewed.

4. The task of identifying suitable candidates, and of subsequently interviewing those selected, should be delegated to a small but representative Selection Committee. The Committee should consist of five members (certainly no more than seven), and should always include the ordained leader, for he or she will be chiefly responsible for envisioning the community with whatever the architect or consultant eventually comes up with. Furthermore, the ordained leader will usually be 'carrying the can' and be acting as 'client' on a day to day basis once the project is under way.

'Architects, Diocesan Advisory Committees and those who work alongside them are called to a radical and prophetic ministry by proactively creating buildings which express the life at the heart of the gospel.'
Peter Cavanagh, *Church Buildings*, p. 3

5. The candidates for interview should be selected on the basis of their previous work, and buildings they have designed or renovated should if possible be visited and experienced by the Selection Committee. Obviously, previous experience of work on church buildings is a great advantage, but is not the only criterion. A flair for design and for creating exciting and delightful interior spaces is what the Committee is after, and as this is such a rare gift, it should be seized upon, whatever the field of experience of the architect concerned.

6. Where needed, advice as to names of suitably experienced architects can be obtained from the Diocesan Advisory Committee (or equivalent body) and, in England, from the Regional Branch of the Royal Institute of British Architects.

7. It is essential that the selected candidates should be invited to attend for interview on clearly defined terms and on an equal footing. Normally travelling expenses

are the only cost to the church council at this stage, but the level of travelling expenses can vary so widely that this should be agreed beforehand to avoid misunderstanding. The candidates should be invited to view the building at their own convenience, but this should be at their own expense, as will be the cost of any illustrative material they choose to present at the interview.

8. In order to be fair to all candidates, all the interviews should be held on the same evening, with a clearly defined timetable which is strictly adhered to. Candidates should have a minimum of 45 minutes each including time for questions.

9. The committee should aim to conclude their deliberations on the same evening, while all three candidates are fresh in their minds. A consensus should be sought whenever possible, but where a casting vote is necessary, it should be exercised by the person who will be having to work most closely with the successful candidate once the project is under way.

10. The selection process will often be an extremely difficult one, especially when the committee feels itself faced with choosing between three equally competent professionals each with a proven track record in liturgical design. In such circumstances, the committee must follow its hunch, for in the final analysis the 'chemistry' between professional and client group will be the deciding factor. The ability to form a team and to work together over a long period is of overriding importance.

Appendix E

DEVELOPING AN OPERATIONAL PLAN

1. An operational plan can enable an organisation to address the following questions:
- where are we now?
- where do we want to be?
- how will we get there?
- what happened?

2. In developing an operational plan, six key questions can be identified:
- what is our mission?
- who are the people we are aiming to serve?
- what are our objectives?
- what is our current role?
- what may be our new role?
- what do we need to improve?

3. Summary of key stages:
(a) where are we now?
- what theological principles underpin our activities?
- what is the purpose of what we do?
- what is our assessment of the current situation:
  (i) in numerical strength
  (ii) in spiritual maturity
- what information do we require?
- what are our limitations and constraints?
- which population group are we aiming at in our outreach?
- are we reaching them?
- in what areas are we least effective?

(b) where do we want to be?
  - what theological model is appropriate for our community?
  - what is our primary role in relation to our local community?
  - what is our dream for our church community in 10 years' time?

(c) how will we get there?
  - how can we improve our performance in these areas?
  - what activities should we limit or discontinue?
  - what is the theological justification for the activities which consume most of our time and energy?
  - what are our options?
  - what are appropriate targets for growth?
  - how do we make this plan a reality?
  - how do we inform and mobilise the church community?
  - how do we communicate our plan to the community we serve?

(d) what happened?
  - how do we monitor our development in relation to targets set?
  - what reports or other documents are required to set out clearly what is happening to us?
  - how can we feed back this experience in order to strengthen our church life and improve our effectiveness?
  - how can we involve the whole church community in assessment of the current situation and in future development?

(e) Yes, but . . . !
  - consider carefully the factors which inhibit growth
  - distinguish factors beyond the church community's control, e.g. government legislation, unemployment, demography, from those which are manageable, e.g. reactive management

under-funding, unclear objectives, obstruction-by-committee, low morale.

4. Tools of the trade:

(a) SWOT analysis will help us assess current situation and available options:
    STRENGTHS / WEAKNESSES / OPPORTUNITIES / THREATS

(b) consideration of key trends in culture and in the Church will throw light on what is happening to us.

(c) analysis of statistics (attendance, recruitment, financial giving).

(d) ministry analysis (what in commerce or local government is called a customer/service matrix) i.e. who is getting what service, and how ministry time is related to theological priorities.

5. The above notes represent merely a skeletal outline of the stages in operational planning. Further details of this process in a Local Government context in the UK are contained in the document *Service Planning*, published by the Personnel Services Department of Kirklees Metropolitan Council, Civic Centre I, Huddersfield, HD1 2NF.

Appendix F

FUNDRAISING

1. Start with prayer – and approach the Boss with a truly open mind, knowing that one of the options is to close down this particular factory.

2. If you get the go-ahead, start with the worshipping congregation. If they are not willing to give sacrificially, then forget the whole thing.

3. Make sure also your parish is clearly seen to be giving away (at least 10% of net income) in the same manner as you hope to receive from others – 'give and it shall be given to you'.

4. Go for direct giving over a short period (six weeks) to determine whether we are in business. Guarantee no jumble sales, fetes or sponsored swims, in exchange for generous cheques on the table.

5. The congregation also needs to let go of brass eagles and favourite pews; unless they are willing to sell off everything except items they are actually going to use, then again, forget it. We cannot expect others to give generously if we are holding on to valuable but useless possessions. Old furniture from church buildings has a considerable retail value, the highest prices being obtained through placing advertisements in local newspapers (rather than using dealers).

6. Examine what assets in the way of land or buildings can be thrown into the pot. For example, a church hall site or piece of waste ground may be sold off. A church field may appear 'essential', but examine how often the church community actually uses it, and then

Refurbished pendant fittings, Bath Abbey

decide whether it is a luxury which will have to be relinquished.

7. Consult bodies advising charities on trust funds available, who may be able to advise you of equivalent bodies in other parts of the country.

8. Submit well designed project leaflet (neither scrappy nor flashy) to appropriate charities with as much information as possible, geared to their particular interests. Annual accounts need to be included.

9. Most trusts will be interested only in the Church as an agent of community service and renewal, and it needs to be shown that your completed scheme will be of clear benefit to local community groups, especially the disadvantaged. It is essential to have supporting letters of intent from prospective users (e.g. Social Services and Health Authority), not just expressions of pious hope.

10. Plug into contacts from the given-ness of your situation:
e.g. – write to every other church in your country with the same dedication (and respond generously to them when it's their turn!)
– write to other churches affiliated to the same organisations as your own, and to the organisations themselves
– approach churches in your twin town or in a town of the same name on the other side of the Atlantic
– approach another church in a different type of environment with a view to forging a link

11. Every parish has its own story, a famous son, or a quirk of history which gives you an angle. Discover it and use it for all it's worth!

12. Finally, remember that the money always follows the vision. Where there is no vision, the projects perish; where there is true vision which is of God, finance will follow as surely as night follows day.

Appendix G

INSTALLATION OF NEW LIGHTING SCHEMES

St Mark, Harrogate;
James Thorp, 1988

'It's my opinion that electricity spoils our service.'

Algot the sexton, to the priest.
Winter Light, Ingmar
Bergman, 1962

1. Identify which areas in the church you wish to highlight (where the liturgical action takes place), and give them first priority.

2. Light these areas with spots, not floods, with fittings (preferably concealed) as near as possible to the objects concerned; e.g. to light a nave altar, position the spots behind a rood beam or capital, or in a corona suspended above the altar.

3. Establish two levels of lighting (or more with dimmer switches), with one setting for liturgical use, and one for other occasions when a single spot softly picks out one or two features.

4. For the remainder of the church it is important to create contrast with the highly-lit focal points. RESIST PRESSURE FOR OVERLIGHTING! 100 to 150 lux is quite adequate for a seating area.

The needs of those with poor eyesight must not be forgotten, but can usually be met by encouraging those concerned to apply common sense when choosing a place to sit (as would those with a hearing disability). As with the design of sound systems, the needs of the minority should not subject the majority to unnecessarily high levels of provision throughout a building.

'When it comes to the placement of the electric fittings, they should preferably not be any higher than an armslength above the head.'

Jerk Alton, *The Lighting of Churches*

'The light should thus be directed downwards and shielded from view in order to obtain satisfying reading light and, at the same time, preserve the architectural qualities of the churchroom.'

Jerk Alton, *The Lighting of Churches*

5. For general seating areas therefore, light fittings should be:

(i) positioned as LOW as possible – using pendant or wall-mounted fittings – to give intimacy and for easy maintenance. In small spaces, lamps can be placed on the floor. The French even insert light fittings *in* the floor, but then, they know all about sexy liturgical space!

(ii) directed DOWNWARDS, to make maximum use of power used, and to 'cosify' the building by reducing its apparent height and volume.

6. Let church ceilings look after themselves. Uplighting is much overdone and should only be used when you have a really special feature to illuminate, e.g. a painted ceiling, and even then only sparingly. A single PAR 38 fitting is sufficient for a whole chancel roof.

7. Fluorescent tubes are fit only for kitchens and should be outlawed from worship areas 'at all times and in all places'.

8. Consult your electrical supplier about high efficiency bulbs and low voltage fittings; these can save you money.

Taizé

Appendix H

FLOOR SURFACES

Hard Surfaces
Hard surfaces are particularly appropriate for areas within the liturgical space which are in some way 'set apart' as being of special significance, e.g. the spaces immediately surrounding altar-table or ambo.

Every effort should be made to uncover floors of quality (e.g. tiled sanctuaries) buried beneath seas of blue or red carpet.

Where new work is being carried out, hard surfaces of quality will give to the alterations a sense of dignity and permanence. Muted materials appropriate to the area (e.g. stone from a local quarry, or bricks from a local yard) should always be used in preference to more exotic materials which, despite their cost, can appear cheap and flashy. Timber is an alternative quality finish appropriate to particular areas of liturgical significance, but can suffer from the creak factor and is usually more noisy to walk over than stone. Used throughout a church building, it can give a rather cold and unwelcoming effect.

(b) Carpeting and Matting
Carpeting or matting is particularly appropriate to the main areas of assembly, where the majority of the community sit and move about.

Although a relatively new feature in church interiors, carpeting or matting can do much to unify the place where the liturgical assembly gathers, can reduce noise, can contribute to a feeling of warmth and intimacy, and can also provide 'overflow seating' for young people.

At the same time, carpeting can affect the acoustics of a church building and, where an unsuitable choice is made, can seriously detract from the interior as a place of prayer and worship. However, the prejudice against carpeted church interiors on the part of certain 'purists' should be guarded against.

The following points need to be borne in mind:

1. The carpet is not a feature in its own right, but a *background* upon which the colour and movement of the liturgical action is set. Strong colours (e.g. the traditional red or blue) and patterns of any kind are therefore to be avoided.* Neutral colours only are appropriate, e.g. pale green, stone, beige etc. The warm muted colour of matting from natural fibres is particularly appropriate liturgically.

2. While a hard wearing carpet is obviously desirable, it should also be comfortable enough to encourage worshippers, where kneeling is the custom, to kneel on the carpet and not on kneelers. Where possible, the use of kneelers should be discontinued once a church is carpeted, as the clash of colours detracts from the liturgical action and from the visual unity of the interior harmony.

3. Carpet tiles sound an attractive proposition but never give an entirely satisfactory a finish as traditional carpeting, and should be avoided.

4. Before laying carpet, the floor area in question should be tested for rising damp, and the backing chosen accordingly. Your inspecting architect's comments should be sought as to what kind of carpet

* In a consistory court held at Hoylandswaine in September 1997, the Chancellor of the Wakefield Diocese, Peter Collier Q.C., ruled against the PCC in its petition for the introduction of a blue carpet, on the grounds that 'if a carpet is dominant it speaks of itself and draws attention to itself . . . away from the other features of a church that speak of the message and sacraments of the gospel'.

backing is appropriate to the floor surface in question. Rubber backed carpet should be avoided because of its tendency to sweat.

5. An excellent advice booklet, *Church Floors and Floor Coverings*, is available from the Council for the Care of Churches, Fielden House, Little College Street, London, SW1P 3SH. Tel: 0171 222 3793.

6. Some floor coverings, when involved in fire, may react to produce large volumes of heat and smoke, thereby presenting a hazard to the means of escape. In England, new coverings should comply with British Standard 5287, and if in doubt, expert advice should be sought.

Appendix I

'THE HERITAGE TRAIL': SOME CONSERVATION ISSUES

Ice-cream parlours and
tourist trails . . .

No book on the subject of re-ordering our church buildings can get away with avoiding (though attempted in the first edition!) the conservation issue i.e. how far can we go in adapting historic buildings to meet contemporary needs without despoiling them? The Church in England faces tremendous pressure to leave its buildings untouched, both from without – from pressure groups protecting various periods or aspects of our architectural heritage, and from within – from worshippers who see the Church as a bastion against change, not an agency to bring it about.

In the final analysis, the issue has probably more to do with the internal than the external pressures i.e. with theology rather than architecture, and a clue to this is provided by the experience of mainstream churches in the United States where, though short on history, congregations can be long on reactionary and protective attitudes to changes in their worship spaces.

Whilst this topic should really be the subject of a whole book, I offer the following comments on the situation in England:

1. As guardians of so many buildings of priceless historic and architectural value, the Church is beholden to the rest of the nation to treasure them, so long as they remain in use for Christian worship. We should approach our historic buildings in gratitude to God for the work of past generations, with delight and with the deepest respect, even a certain nervousness, but not with a reverence that borders on idolatory.

2. The Church must continue to proclaim that the greatest treasure it guards is that contained within these glorious buildings i.e. the community of faith that inhabits them and uses them, and which lives out a theological identity as the Body of Christ in the world today. The community of faith is the picture, the building the frame.

3. This theological truth leads to the realisation that historic buildings designed for worship are dynamic rather that static structures; they cannot be frozen in time. They are organic structures, continually evolving over the centuries as they have been adapted again and again to accommodate fresh needs or new ideas. Their walls bear the marks, not only of celebration and renewal, but also of cruelty and despoilation. All these aspects form part of our Christian story, to our glory or our shame.

4. Although church buildings are therefore just like any other buildings in that they have an architectural shape and character, they are not *primarily* architectural forms. They are rather theological statements in stone or brick about the living community of faith that has become synonymous with them, a community of faith that is continually developing and changing. The theologically unhelpful custom of using the same word 'church' to denote both community and building indicates just how inextricably the two are bound together. We must try very hard to get this message across to those who see church buildings as architecture alone, of which the churches are perceived as unworthy stewards.

5. The conservation of historic church buildings is therefore a proper concern for the Church, for a well-maintained building is like a well-kept diary; through better understanding the past, we are enabled to live more fully in the present. Conservation for the Church will mean the continuance of the ancient and unbroken Christian tradition of adapting our buildings to meet contemporary needs. Changed needs arise from

both growth and decline, from fresh theological insights concerning the relationship between God and humankind, and from the rediscovery of the New Testament concept of the whole assembly of faith as the priesthood of the New Covenant.

6. Such adaptation was carried out in past generations with ruthless and uncompromising thoroughness, with an apparently total disregard for the past, and we should not lose sight of the fact that the end result of these cathartic changes is precisely that melange of styles and materials that all of us, including protectionists, now find so delightful.

7. It would however be totally inappropriate for the Church today to embark on a similar programme, even if free to do so. We are today more aware of our heritage and of the irreperable damage done in the past e.g. by over-enthusiastic 'restorers' of the last century who obliterated almost every medieval parish church in the country.

8. The task of conservation needs therefore to be approached with great sensitivity and with a deep respect for all that is of excellence from past generations. Any prayerful Christian community with a sense of history and of the communion of saints should be eager to delight in its story and to maintain visible links with the past. We are a pilgrim people who must never forget the previous stages of our journey.

9. The delicate task of deciding what goes and what stays, at which point the needs of contemporary liturgy must take precedence over the retention of previous layouts or structures, should be a slow and careful one combining:
(a) prayer and study over a lengthy period,* including an informed examination of our own heritage of evolving worship and Christian life.

* A six-week study course is offered in Appendix J.

(b) discussions with representatives of the wider church to see what is happening elsewhere, to understand prevailing trends and the theological principles behind them

(c) discussions with the local community to better understand its perception of the church and its building, their expectations and needs

(d) discussions with the statutory heritage bodies and with period-specific societies* likely to have a special interest in the building concerned, to try and establish a forum for consultation at an early stage

(e) involvement of an external *animateur* who will attempt to draw together these different strands to enable the outline sketch of an appropriate scheme to emerge

10. It is of course impossible to suggest generally applicable guidelines about where to draw the line between past and present, between history and liturgy, for the answer will be different in every individual case, and there is no right or wrong answer. Nevertheless we can, from the Church's point of view, say that, if in doubt, there will always remain a presumption for change, because that is our story. The much quoted Maidstone Judgement (1994) might suggest otherwise, but it is gainsaid every week by new re-ordering schemes up and down the country as the Church renews and re-equips itself and its buildings. The Law is usually busy locking the stable door after the horse has bolted, and re-ordering is no exception.

11. We must strive however to ensure that such renewal proceeds, if at all possible, without the exhausting, painful and potentially costly ordeal of litigation. Any community of faith considering a re-ordering scheme needs to make friends with both statutory and voluntary bodies working in the same field, to present

* *'The National Amenity Societies': their role in the conservation of Anglich churches.* This guide, issued in 1998, can be obtained from The Council for the Care of Churches.

a well argued case for change, and to sit down with all those concerned, including potential objectors, to try and work out a common approach.

12. What is absolutely non-negotiable for the Church is that preservation is not an option. It is difficult if not impossible to conceive of a church building which will not require improvement and reordering of some kind if it is to serve effectively as the 'local centre for worship and mission' of a developing Christian community. There will be exceptions: buildings that are classic period pieces that it would be a crime to disturb. In such cases, the question for the church is whether these buildings remain suitable for regular use for worship, or whether they should be vested in the Churches Conservation Trust, or used occasionally for special events, the community of faith transferring its regular liturgy to other more conducive premises.

13. The bottom line for the Church is that, should events conspire to prevent a community of faith from adapting an historic church building for present day needs, then it should withdraw from the building and set in motion the redundancy procedure. In the Consistory Court held at St Aidan's, Birmingham in March 1998, the Bishop of Birmingham made it clear to the Court that, should the imaginative scheme for the reordering of St Aidan's be refused, then the living Church would not be able to go on using these dead stones.

14. A final word on what is known misleadingly as 'ecclesiastical exemption' from Listed Building Consent to alter the interiors of our church buildings – misleading because, of course, such alterations are subject to a separate system of control under the Faculty Jurisdiction, running parallel to the planning system administered by the local authority. While it is certainly true that it is a privilege for local churches to have their proposals scrutinised and determined by others within the Church, setting out from the same starting point, it is less of a privilege if there are

objections to the scheme. At this point the Faculty Jurisdiction seems to fall over backwards to accommodate the objector, and the threat of a Consistory Court is sufficient to deter many a church council from continuing with its long-cherished scheme. Although there is much dark talk of the awful fate that awaits the English churches devoid of Faculty Jurisdiction, I would simply wish to comment that in such an event it may well be those who are opposed to change who would cry longest into their soup.

Appendix J

A SIX-WEEK CRASH COURSE ON THE DESIGN OF LITURGICAL SPACE

Week One: Tent or Temple?

Preparation
Read and find out what you can about:
  Numbers 9.15–end
  1 Samuel 7.1–13
  2 Chronicles 6.18–21

Group session
1. Discuss the tension between tent and temple, nomadic and static traditions, evident within these readings and within the Old Testament as a whole.

2. What was the attitude of Jesus to the Temple in his day? Compare Mark 11.15–17 with Mark 13.1–2.

3. At what points in the life of our own community of faith is there evidence of tension between the tent and temple aspects of our worship and our life together?

4. Which aspect do we think is closest to the insights and teaching of Jesus of Nazareth?

5. How can we give clearer expression to this priority in our worship?

Practical task
Arrange to hold the main Sunday liturgy in a different setting, preferably for a limited period e.g. during Lent.

Afterwards assess to what extent this experience has informed our understanding of the Church as a pilgrim people, and of liturgy as an encounter with God.

Week Two: The Environment of Change
Preparation
Read:
  James 4.13–14
  Hebrews 13.12–14

Group session
1. What are the main technological developments that have transformed our way of life since childhood?

2. To what extent has social change affected the concept of our nation as a Christian country? To what extent is the average person aware of the Christian Church in every day life?

3. In what ways is the Church today a different sort of organisation from when we were baptised?

4. In what ways has the experience of worship and of church membership changed over our lifetime?

5. In our society should the Church be primarily a bastion of stability or an agent of change?

Practical task
Arrange to visit and to take part in worship at two other local church communities, one traditional, one progressive. Compare and contrast the experiences.

Week Three: The Church Building
Preparation
Read:
  Luke 4.16
  Luke 9.57–58

Group session
1. Is the common use of the same word to describe both the community of faith and the building it meets in helpful or confusing? If confusing, which description should we change, and to what?

2. Is the building the physical structure that gives identity to the community of faith, or merely the frame

around the picture? Do we serve the building or does the building serve us?

3. Is our building in the right place? Is it the right building? Or is it the right building in the right place but unsuitable for present day needs?

4. Where does the shoe pinch? In what ways does our building need overhauling and re-equipping if we are to be liberated in our worship and effective in our work together for God?

5. What should we do about it? Let the ideas flow!

Practical task
Arrange to visit a community of faith, possibly of another tradition, that uses a secular building (e.g. an industrial unit) as its worship centre. In what ways does such a practice help or hinder worship and church growth?

Week Four: The Hospitable Church
Preparation
Read:
   Luke 19.1–5
   Acts 16.14–15
   Revelation 19.6–9

Group session
1. The enjoyment of a meal, of a party, is a constant New Testament theme. How does the experience of coming to visit our community of faith measure up?

2. How might we redesign the entrance to our building to make the experience of encountering our community an easy and happy experience for the newcomer?

3. Do we have the basic facilities e.g. a kitchen and a toilet, to make our hospitality more than a smile and a handshake? If not, what are we going to do about it?

4. What is the first thing that people see when they enter our worship space? What dominates it visually? What should dominate it, if warm and open hospitality is to be the message?

5. What are the obstacles to putting things right?

Practical task
(a) Divide up to visit other church communities, and compare and contrast the welcome you receive.
(b) Invite a small group from another church to take part in your Sunday liturgy, and provide them with a feedback sheet on how hospitable they found you and your worship.

Week Five: The Teaching Church
Preparation
Read:
  Numbers 21.8
  John 12.32

Group session
1. What sign or symbol dominates your worship space, or is it a jumble of confused visual images? What symbol would you wish to predominate? How should it be incorporated into the space?

2. What impression of your community and its worship is given by the arrangement of the principal pieces of liturgical furniture? e.g. is your altar table accessible or distant, on the floor or up steps, open or fenced? Make a similar assessment of lectern/pulpit and font.

3. Is there duplication in the liturgical furniture? Is there more than one altar or font in your worship space, or more than one place for the reading and preaching of the word? If so, what should be done about it?

4. What impression of your community and its worship is given by the seating plan? Does the seating plan

suggest active participation or passive observance? How do the seats for leaders and specialists (e.g. singers) relate to those for the rest of the assembly?

5. Is the font like a 'spring of water welling up to eternal life' (John 4.14), or a dried up well stuck in the corner? How might water be made use of, at the point of entry into the liturgical space as a sign of God's life-giving generosity and of our baptism?

Practical task
Arrange a visit to a recently re-ordered church building and discuss with members of that faith community the differences the scheme has made to their worship.

Week Six: The Transformed Church
Preparation
Read:
  Matthew 17.1–8
  1 Peter 2.9–10

Group session
1. In the light of our exploration over the last five weeks, what is our dream for our worship space? How can it be re-arranged to speak more clearly of the glory of God, of our life together, and of our concern for those outside?

2. In particular, how should the liturgical foci of font, ambo and altar be so arranged as to do justice to who we are and what we have to offer? What is the liturgical sequence that is best for *us*?

3. How urgent a priority for us is the re-ordering of our worship space and building?

4. What are the obstacles to the implementation of a re-ordering scheme?

5. How can we best share 'good news' about the formative process of re-ordering and liturgical renewal?

Practical task
Arrange and plan a Saturday teach-in or a parish weekend away at which the aim will be to envison and mobilise the community of faith in this area of our life.

POSTSCRIPT:
'THE MAGICAL MYSTERY TOUR'

The Californian liturgist, architect and priest, Eliza Linley, sets out in her book, *Holy People, Holy Space*, an educational model for parish leaders. 'The Magical Mystery Tour' is a particularly useful tool in enabling a church leadership to grow in awareness of what they are about in a re-ordering project.

Tate Gallery
St Ives, Cornwall

The important thing is to help people develop a visual and experiential vocabulary of liturgical space. One particularly enjoyable way to do this is to go on a day-long field trip to visit liturgically and spatially interesting sites. The purpose is not only to experience the environments, but to do it together, and to reflect upon those experiences as a group. Note that all these events should be open to the whole community. Spatial awareness helps us to relate to our environment. Particularly in this context, it helps us understand who we are as the people of God. It is in sharing the experience that we reach a common understanding.

It is important, in planning the event, to include non-religious as well as religious places. Qualities of space affect us in certain ways, and we may be less blinded by habit in an environment which has no liturgical associations whatsoever.

Gilbert Ostdiek O.F.M., who developed this exercise in his book, *Catechesis for Liturgy*, describes what participants are to do at each site:

> The first thing to do is to roam around in the space, to take in its sights, smells, colors, textures, and to just get the feel of the space by moving about in it. It is important to remain in each place and to attend to it with our bodily senses until we experience its impact. This cannot be rushed. Once the place has made its impact on us, we can

turn our attention to describing and naming the experience. I recommend that we go on the field trip equipped with three questions . . . First, a descriptive question: what strikes me about this place? Second, a naming question: what feelings does it evoke in me? And third, an application question: if I were to pray here, what would my prayer be? If I were to plan a liturgy for this space, what would it be like?

CONTACTS

The Council for the Care of Churches
Fielden House, Little College Street, London SW1P 3SH. Tel: 0717 222 3793. Fax: 0171 222 3794. Secretary: Dr Thomas Cocke.
The Council is the C of E body which co-ordinates the activities of Diocesan Advisory Committees (42 in number) throughout the country, organises conferences and seminars and publishes a good list of specialised booklets on numerous aspects of church care and conservation.

Methodist Church Property Division
Central Buildings, Oldham Street, Manchester M1 1JU. Tel: 0161 236 5194. Gen. Sec.: Rev Kenneth Street.
Advises on all matters concerning Methodist churches and other property and issues a series of publications dealing with quinquennial inspections, giving scheme procedures, listed buildings, church art and theological principles.

Church of Scotland Advisory Committees on Artistic Matters
121 George Street, Edinburgh EH2 4YN. Tel: 0131 225 5722. Convenor: Mr Gordon Withers.
Publishes a handbook Care for your Church and gives advice on all matters to do with church buildings, furnishings and artwork in The Church of Scotland (Presbyterian).

The Liturgy Office of the Bishops Conference of England and Wales
39 Eccleston Square, London SW1V 1PL. Tel: 0171 821 0553. Assistant secretary: Mr Martin Foster.
The Office advises on all matters concerning the Liturgical arrangement, furnishings and music etc. for RC churches in England and Wales.

Church in Wales
Following the publication of the Report Of The Commission on Faculties (by the Governing Body of the Church in Wales, August 1993) there has been established a central body authorised to oversee all works at Cathedral and Church Sites in Wales. The Cathedrals and Churches Commission is based at 39, Cathedral Road, Cardiff CF1 9XF. Tel: 01222 231638. Fax: 01222 387835. The Chairman is Dr R. Brinley Jones. A handbook on the role of the Commission is forthcoming. For further information please contact the Secretary Paul Rees.

Ecclesiastical Architects' & Surveyors' Association
Hon. Sec.: Mr David Clarke BSc., Scan House, 29 Radnor Cliff, Folkestone, Kent CT20 2JJ. Tel and Fax: 01303 254008.
Founded in 1872 to promote good standards in the design and repair of ecclesiastical buildings, including churches and chapels, halls and houses. Today an expanding organisation with a membership of more than 400, which includes a large proportion of architects and surveyors who hold church appointments. There are three general meetings each year, at which papers are given on specialist subjects and the Association publishes a quarterly newsletter and a series of technical booklets.

Churches National House Coalition
CNHC, Central Buildings, Oldham Street, Manchester M1 1JT. Tel: 0161 236 9321. Fax: 0161 237 5359.
It is apparent that the extent to which affordable housing is even considered, let alone given priority,

when a church site becomes available, varies enormously in different parts of the country and from denomination to denomination. CNHC role is one of taking a national policy overview, and of providing independent advice to local churches (with regard to individual sites) or church authorities (with regard to disposal policies).

CNHC has developed a specialist agency to promote the use of church land and property for affordable housing. The key component of this service will be pre-development advice offered by a network of experienced local advisers.

Church Building
A glossy, bi-monthly magazine featuring projects to renew religious buildings of all Christian traditions as well as other faiths.
Gabriel Communications, St James' Buildings, Manchester M1 8DS. Tel: 0161 236 8856.

Environment and Art
Liturgy Training Publications, 1800 North Hermitage Avenue, Chicago, IL 60622-1101, USA. Tel: 001 (800) 933 4213.

Bibliography

ABRAMOVITZ, Anita, *People and Spaces*, Viking Press, 1979.

ADDLESHAW, G W O & ETCHELLS, Frederick, *The Architectural Setting of Anglican Worship*, Faber, London, 1948.

ALTON, Jerk, *The Lighting of Churches*, privately printed, Sweden, 1993.

ANDERSON, Bernard W, *Living World of the Old Testament*, Longman, 1958.

BARNUM, Barbara, *The Process of Liturgical Change in the USA*, Liturgy North 96.

BRIDGES, William, *Managing Transitions*, Addison-Wesley, 1995.

BROCK, Patrick, *A Theology of Church Design*, Ecclesiastical Architects & Surveyors Association, 1985.

BROOK, Peter, *The Empty Space*, Penguin, London, 1990.

BROWN, Bill, Ed., *Building and Renovation Kit for places of Catholic Worship*, Liturgy Training Publications, Chicago, 1982.

BULLOCH, James, *Pilate to Constantine*, St Andrew Press, 1981.

BUSCEMI, John, *Places for Devotion*, Meeting House Essays No 4, Liturgy Training Publications No. 4, Chicago, 1993.

CAVANAGH, Peter, *Church Buildings*, Liverpool DAC, 1994.

CHINN, Nancy, *Spaces for Spirit*, Liturgy Training Publications, Chicago, 1998.

CLIFTON-TAYLOR, Alec, *English Parish Churches as Works of Art*, Batsford, 1974.

COLE, W Owen, *Six Religions in the Twentieth Century*, Stanley Thornes, 0000.

COPE, Gilbert, Ed., *Making the Building Serve the Liturgy*, Mowbray, London, 1962.

COTTRELL, Stephen, *Sacrament, Wholeness and Evangelism*, Grove Books 1996.

—— *The Re-ordering of Creation*, Liturgy North 96.

CRICHTON, J D, *Christian Celebration: The Mass*, Geoffrey Chapman, 1971.

DART, Susan, *Edward Dart: Architect*, 1993 Evanston Publishing, Evanston IL 60202.

DAVIES, Jon Gower, *The Evangelistic Bureaucrat*, Tavistock, 1972.

DAVRIL, Anselme, *Reforme Liturgique dans un Monastere*, La Maison Dieu No. 192, 1992.

DEBUYST, Frederic, *Modern Architecture & Christian Celebration*, Ecumenical Studies in Worship No. 18, 1968, John Knox Press, Richmond, Va.

—— *Jean Cosse: des maisons pour vivre*, Collection Documents Actuels, Editions art vie esprit, Bruxelles.

—— *Le renouveau de l'Art sacré de 1920 a 1962*, Editions Mame, Paris, 1991.

DIX, Gregory, *The Shape of the Liturgy*, Black 1945.

DOLL, Peter, *After the Primitive Christians: The Eighteenth-Century Anglican Eucharist in its Architectural Setting*, Grove Books, 1997.

ENVIRONMENT & ART IN CATHOLIC WORSHIP, National Conference of Catholic Bishops Liturgical Training Publications, 1986.

FABIAN, Richard, *Worship at St Gregory's*, All Saints Co., 1995.

FAITH IN THE CITY, A Report of the Archbishop of Canterbury's Commission on Urban Priority Areas (Popular Version) 1985.

FOLEY, Edward, *From Age to Age*, Liturgy Training Publications, Chicago, 1991.

HAMMOND, Peter, *Liturgy and Architecture*, Barrie and Rockliff, 1960.

—— *Towards a Church Architecture*, The Architectural Press, 1962.

HELLRIEGEL, Martin, *Unto the Altar*, Nelson, 1963.

HOFFMAN, Lawrence A, *Sacred Places and the Pilgrimage of Life*, Meeting House Essays No. 1. Liturgy Training Publications, Chicago, 1991.

HUCK, Gabe, *Liturgy with Style and Grace*, Liturgy Training Publications, Chicago, 1984.

HUFFMAN & VAN LOON, *Where we Worship*, Augsburg Publishing, Minneapolis, MN 1987.

JENKINS, David E, *God, Miracle and the Church of England*, SCM, 1997.

JOHNSON, Stephen & JOHNSON, Cuthbert, *Planning for Liturgy*, St Michael's Abbey Press, 1983.

JONES, WAINWRIGHT, YARNOLD, Eds, *The Study of Liturgy*, SPCK, London, 1978.

JONES-FRANK, Michael *Iconography & Liturgy*, Meeting House Essay No. 6, Liturgy Training Publications, Chicago, 1994.

JUNG, Carl G (ed.), *Man and His Symbols*, Doubleday, 1964.

KAMARCIK, Frank, *The Berakah Award for 1981*, Worship, Vol. 55, No. 4, July 1981. (Organ of the North American Academy of Liturgy.)

KING, Charles A, *Monasticism in the Twentieth Century*, Journal of the American Society for Church Architecture, April 1971, No. 11.

KIRKLEES Metropolitan Council, *Service Planning*, Kirklees Personnel Services, 1993.

KUEHN, Regina, *A Place for Baptism*, Liturgy Training Publications, Chicago, 1992.

KUNG, Hans, *Christianity: The Religious Situation of our Time*, SCM Press, 1995.

—— *Why I am still a Christian*, T & T Clark, 1987.

LANE, George & KEZYS, Algimantas, *Chicago Churches and Synagogues*, Loyola University Press, Chicago, 1981.

LANGER, Susanne, *Feeling and Form*, Routledge and Kegan Paul, 1953.

LARSON, George A & PRIDMORE, Jay, *Chicago Architecture & Design*, 1993 Harry N Abrams Inc., New York.

LEONARD, John K and MITCHELL, Nathan D, *The Postures of the Assembly During the Eucharistic Prayer*, Liturgy Training Publications, Chicago, 1994.

LINDSTROM, Randall S, *Creativity and Contradiction*, 'European Churches since 1970', American Institute of Architects Press, Washington DC, 1987.

LINLEY, Eliza, *Holy People, Holy Space*, privately printed, 1990.

MAGUIRE, Robert & MURRAY, Keith, *Modern Churches of the World*, Dutton Vista Pictureback, 1965.

MAGUIRE, Robert, *The Re-ordering of Churches: what is it to be radical?* Liturgy North, 1996.

MARSHALL, Michael, *Free to Worship*, Marshall Pickering, London, 1996.

MAUCK, Marchita B, *Places for worship: A guide to building and renovating*, Liturgical Press, Collegeville, MN 1995.

—— *Shaping a House for the Church*, Liturgy Training Publications, Chicago, 1990.

MAXTONE GRAHAM, Ysenda, *The Church Hesitant*, Hodder and Stoughton, London, 1994.

NELSON, Gertrud Mueller, *To Dance with God*, Paulist Press, New Jersey, 1986.

NEWBIGIN, Lesslie, *The Gospel in a Pluralist Society*, SPCK, London, 1989.

NIEBLING, Howard V, 'Monastic Churches Erected by American Benedictines Since World War II. Part Two: Churches built during and after Vatican Council II,' *American Benedictine Review*, Sept. 1975.

O'CONNELL, Marvin, *Critics on Trial*, Catholic University of America Press, 1994.

O'CONNOR, John, *Why Revive the Liturgy, and How?* Privately printed, 1935.

PATTERNS FOR WORSHIP, A Report by the Liturgical Commission of the General Synod of the Church of England, GS 898, London, 1989.

PATTISON, George, *Art, Modernity and Faith*, SCM Press, London, 1991.

PHILIPPART, David, *Saving Signs and Wondrous Words*, Liturgy Training Publications, Chicago, 1996.

POLLAN, Michael, *A Place of My Own*, Bloomsbury, London, 1997.

POTTEBAUM, Gerard A, *The Rites of People*, Pastoral Press, 1992.

PROULX, E Annie, *The Shipping News*, Fourth Estate, London, 1993.

PURDY, Martin, *Churches and Chapels: Design & Development Guides*, Butterworth Architecture, 1991.

REINHOLD, H A, *The Dynamics of Liturgy*, Macmillan, 1961.

RYAN, G Thomas, *The Sacristy Manual*, Liturgy Training Publications, Chicago, 19??.

SCHILLEBEECKX, Edward, *God the Future of Man*, Sheed and Ward, 1968.

SEASOLTZ, Kevin, *The House of God: Sacred Art and Church Architecture*, Herder & Herder, New York, 1963.

SHANDS, Alfred, *The Liturgical Movement and the Local Church*, SCM Press, 1965.

SIMONS, Thomas G and FITZPATRICK, James M, *The Ministry of Liturgical Environment*, Liturgical Press, Collegeville, 1984.

SOVIK, E A, *Architecture for Worship*, Augsburg Publishing House, Minneapolis, MN, 1973.

STANIFORTH, Maxwell (trans.), *Early Christian Writings*, Penguin, London, 1968.

THE PLACE OF WORSHIP, Irish Episcopal Commission for Liturgy, Veritas, 1991.

VATICAN COUNCIL II: Vol I The Conciliar and Postconciliar Documents, New Revised Edition, Austin Flannery (ed.), Costello, 1996.

VERMES, Geza, *Jesus the Jew*, SCM Press, 1973.

WARREN, Robert, *Building Missionary Congregations*, Church House Publishing, London, 1995.

Index